Why can't computer books be easier to understand?

Not all of us want to become computer professionals, but we do want to have fun with our computers and be productive. The new *Simple Guides* cover the popular topics in computing. Most importantly, they are simple to understand. Each book in the series introduces the main features of a topic and shows you how to get the most from your PC.

Simple Guides – No gimmicks, no jargon, no fuss

Available in the *Simple Guides* series:

The Internet

Searching the Internet

The PC

Office 2000

Windows 98

E-commerce

Digital cameras, scanning and using images

Internet research

Building a website

Using spreadsheets

Using email

Putting audio and video on your website

Dreamweaver 4

Flash 5

A simple guide to

writing for your website

Susannah Ross

An imprint of PEARSON EDUCATION

Pearson Education Limited

Head Office:
Edinburgh Gate
Harlow
Essex CM20 2JE
Tel: +44 (0)1279 623623
Fax: +44 (0)1279 431059

London Office:
128 Long Acre
London WC2E 9AN
Tel: +44 (0)20 7447 2000
Fax: +44 (0)20 7240 5771

First published in Great Britain 2001
© Susannah Ross 2001

The right of Susannah Ross to be identified as the Author of this Work have been asserted by her in accordance with the Copyright, Designs and Patents Act 1988.

ISBN 0-130-41557-X

British Library Cataloguing in Publication Data
A CIP catalogue record for this book can be obtained from the British Library.

Many of the designations used by manufacturers and sellers to distinguish their products are claimed as trademarks. Pearson Education Limited has made every attempt to supply trademark information about manufacturers and their products mentioned in this book.

10 9 8 7 6 5 4 3 2 1

Typeset by Pantek Arts Ltd, Maidstone, Kent
Printed and bound in Great Britain by Ashford Colour Press, Gosport, Hampshire

The publishers' policy is to use paper manufactured from sustainable forests.

Contents

Introduction

It's the words that matter. Research into how people use the Web repeatedly shows that the words used on a website are crucial to its success. It seems obvious when you think about it. Yet we are so preoccupied with the colour, the design, the links and the layout that the question 'What is the site going to say?' is often the last thing we consider.

Successful sites are those with a clear purpose, clearly expressed. They contain the right amount of information, and are well structured and presented. Many websites fail because they have not been properly thought out or carefully written. They do not communicate well with the user or give the relevant information.

The Web is a demanding medium for writers. You have a few seconds in which to get the user's interest and you can lose it very quickly; you have to organise your material quite differently from the way you would for a printed publication; and your product is never finished. This Simple Guide will help you understand the medium you are writing for and meet those demands. It will take you through the process of writing for the Web step by step, giving you techniques for tackling individual tasks, useful examples of what works and what doesn't, and a reminder of the basic rules of written English.

Whether you are starting from scratch or maintaining an existing site, you can keep the Simple Guide by your side and consult it as you go along.

About the author

Susannah Ross is an Associate of the writing company Clarity (see www.clarity4words.co.uk or contact Susannah@clarity4words.co.uk) and an Associate Trainer with BBC New Media Training.

She was a BBC journalist for 20 years and in her last post as Deputy Editor of World Service News was responsible for recruiting and training journalists and producing the newsroom Style Book.

With Julia Swann, Susannah set up the Select Ideas website for small businesses and individual enterprises (www.selectideas.co.uk).

What's so special about the Web?

A whole new world

Lessons for writers

This chapter describes the characteristics of the Web as a medium. It looks at the way websites work and what that means for writers. These are the ideas that inform the advice in this Simple Guide.

Look at a book. Then look at the home page of a website on your screen. With the book, the whole thing is there in your hand. One glance at the cover and the size and shape of it tells you what kind of book it is. You can thumb through more than 150 pages in less than a minute to see whether it is what you want. You are scanning several hundred words a second. If you look for something in particular, it will probably take you a couple of minutes to find and read the words you want.

Compare that with a website (Figure 1.1). When you look at the home page, you have no idea how many pages there are and only a vague idea of what sort of site it is. Once you start looking, you can usually see only one page at a time. You may have at most a few dozen words on the screen. It's rather like using a magnifying glass to read a road atlas: you can clearly see only the small part under the glass; you cannot see the whole page, let alone the whole atlas. With a website, you depend on the site itself to tell you where you are and how to find your way around. So the organisation of the site and the words it uses to explain itself are crucial. All the more so when you consider that a book is a finite object, whereas a website is infinite. It can grow and change all the time.

A website does not work in straight lines. You may dip in and out of this book, or read the contents in a variety of orders, but it is written with a beginning, a middle and an end. Its pages are numbered in sequence. A website has a sort of beginning, in the form of a home page, but there is no guarantee that that's the page you will see first. When you arrive at a page, it has no numerical relationship to the rest of the site. Again, you rely on the site itself to tell you where you are.

All this is by way of explaining why the Web is such a demanding medium to write for. There's more to come. We've had hundreds of years to work out how to write books and barely ten years to work out how to write for websites. We are still in the early stages of this medium.

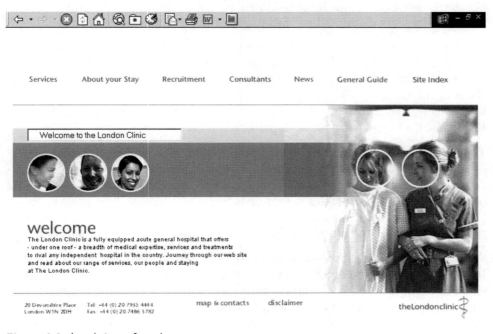

Figure 1.1 A website at first glance.

A whole new world

The World Wide Web (its full name, hence www) is part of the Internet, which was originally a United States military communication network. The World Wide Web was set up in the early 1990s to enable academics to have access to one another's research. It was invented to share information. What makes it unique as a medium is its ability to link information from anywhere to anywhere.

Once people were able to read other people's documents on their own computers, they began to think of all kinds of things they could do with other people through this new medium. Not only could they share ideas with someone in the next room or a continent away, they could make contact and do business with one another in many different ways. The Web is essentially an interactive medium. Relationships – academic, political, personal and commercial – are at its core.

The sharing and the linking, the interactivity, are what make the Web different from other media. Broadcasters talk about producing and transmitting programmes, delivery systems and so on. In other words, it's one-way traffic. The broadcaster decides what the viewer or listener will receive. The programme is linear. The audience are passive, unable to skip the bits that don't interest them or to go back to something that was puzzling or particularly pleasing.

When you read a book, magazine or newspaper you are rather more in control. If you are in a book shop or at a newspaper stand, you can see quite quickly, there and then, what each publication has to offer. Once you've made your choice, you can decide where to begin, what to skip and what to re-read. As a reader of a printed publication you are already much more active than when you watch or listen to a broadcast.

Now compare those experiences with using the Web. You go to the Web for a purpose. You want information, to buy something, to ask advice, to exchange views or to make contact with someone. You may want to listen to music, if you have a sound system on your computer. You might want to see some pictures, although the quality is almost certainly not as good as on a television set. Besides, you are sitting at a desk using a keyboard. You are active and purposeful. If you wanted to watch pictures or listen to music, you'd be more comfortable on the sofa. That is why this Simple Guide calls people who use the Web users, not an audience and not readers.

Users are active. They want something. If one site does not give it to them, they have, theoretically, a choice of about 15 million others. The number is growing all the time. More and more people are getting online and more and more people are setting up sites. So when you write for a website, you are competing with millions for the user's attention. What is more, being online costs money in the United Kingdom and most other European countries. One of the reasons for the rapid growth of Internet use in the United States was that local telephone calls were free. Here, not only do users have an enormous choice of sites, they do not want to waste time if they are paying for it by the minute. They are demanding and impatient.

They can demand something at any time of the day or night. A website has no time of broadcast, time of going to print or day of publication. For the user it exists at the moment that they want it. Because it can be changed or updated at any time, users tend to expect that it will be. There's another reason why they are impatient.

Once they are in a site, they can choose where to go. They don't necessarily start at the home page. They don't necessarily choose the first link that is offered. They may follow several links or none at all. This requires the writer to make clear the identity of the site on each page and the relationship of each page to the rest.

There's another point about how people use the Web. Most people prefer reading on paper in a comfortable chair to reading on a screen sitting at a desk. Not only can you thumb through a book quickly, you can decide where to read it, how to hold it in the best light and what is the right distance from your eyes. Reading on a screen is not a particularly comfortable activity. You have little control over the position of the text or your position at the desk. As it's not comfortable, it is not a very efficient way of obtaining information.

Finally there is the screen itself. Compared with paper, the screen is a crude vehicle for words and pictures. The resolution on a screen is much lower than in print. Images – photographs, drawings and so on – are reproduced less precisely than they are on paper and the same goes for the letters that make up your words. These are yet more reasons for the writer to make it as easy as possible for the user.

Lessons for writers

A website cannot be seen as a whole at one glance. It can be any size and it could go on growing for ever. It is infinite.

Lesson for writers: Your site must be well organised and clearly explained.

A website does not work in straight lines. It is non-linear. It doesn't really have a beginning, much less an end.

Lesson for writers: Every part of your site must explain itself and its relationship to the whole.

The Web is interactive. It is about relationships.

Lesson for writers: Your writing must be conversational.

People go to the Web for a purpose. They want something. They are 'users'.

Lesson for writers: Think of what the user is hoping to get from your site rather than what you want to say.

There are millions of sites competing for their attention.

Lesson for writers: Be brief and tell the user what you are offering straight away.

Being on line costs money.

Lesson for writers: Be clear and concise. Don't waste the user's time.

Reading on a screen is not a comfortable activity.

Lesson for writers: Make it as easy as possible.

Screens are not as efficient as paper as vehicles for words or images.

Lesson for writers: Think about presentation.

What is your website for?

Sorting out your ideas

Before you write anything you should ask yourself 'Why am I writing this, who is it for and what is it about?' This chapter deals with the first question and contains exercises to help you plan your site.

Clear writing is the result of clear thinking. Don't be surprised at the number of stages the Simple Guide suggests you go through before putting finger to keyboard. Resist the temptation to go straight to a screen, and get some bits of paper instead. The time you spend thinking, playing with ideas, scribbling and crossing things out will pay dividends later. It's much easier to change something on a piece of paper than on a website.

Sorting out your ideas

Talking to people is another good way of sorting out your ideas. Try them on a few people, individually or in a group. You will have to explain your ideas, briefly at first, then in more detail if they ask you questions. If they challenge you, you will have to defend your ideas. Talking about them methodically will help you discard ideas that may not work and rethink others. It may also give you new ones.

In any writing, you should start by asking yourself three questions: Why am I writing? For whom? and About what? So start with the first one and ask yourself what your website is for. Even if you are working on a site that is not yours alone, thinking about what it is for will focus your writing. Try this list.

My site exists to:

- share ideas with people who have the same interest as me;
- allow people to find out about me or my business at any time;
- sell products;
- get feedback from customers;

- get useful information and opinions from other people;
- put members of my extended family in touch with one another;
- create a community;
- show that we are accountable to those who fund us;
- make me feel good;
- educate people;
- make my boss feel good;
- make my colleagues feel good;
- communicate with suppliers more cheaply;
- try some exciting animations;
- etc.

The list could go on and on. There are so many things a website can do. Because of that, you need to be clear which are the things that matter. If you can achieve the same result some other way, do so. Websites are time-consuming. They are fun and they may be very effective, but they create a lot of work.

They also set up expectations. All the more reason for you to be clear about what yours is for and, just as important, what it's not for. Remember the busy user, spending money to read words uncomfortably. How irritating to come to a site that describes a wonderful place to hold a party and doesn't tell you how to book it! It is better to promise less, and deliver, than to disappoint.

If you look around the Web, it's not surprising that the most successful sites tend to be those with a clear purpose. The narrower your focus, the easier it is. So if your purpose is to sell a specific product, such as books or holidays, or to provide people with regular access to a particular kind of news or advice, you have a better chance of making your site work than if you just think it's a good idea to have a website.

Many people talk about setting up a website or having one. They don't talk often enough about running or managing one. Having a website is not like having a book or film to show people, it is more like having a farm. The question is not so much 'What is in it?' or 'What does it look like' but 'What does it do?' A website can live and grow. It will flourish if it is used and refreshed and fertilised with new information and ideas. If it is not used, it becomes stale. If the links are not checked regularly they may no longer work – they 'rot'. The site withers and eventually dies.

If you are setting up a new site or revamping an existing one (Table 2.1):

- think of all the things your site could do;
- write each one down on a separate piece of paper;
- for each one write down why you want to do it;
- for each one write down how the site will do it;
- for each one write down why a website will do it better than it's done now;
- put them in order of importance;
- discard as many as you can;
- describe the purpose of your site in a single line (3–10 words).

Table 2.1 The questions to ask when setting up a website.

What?	Why?	How?	Why better on the Web?	Order of importance
Make our company more efficient	We want to reduce costs	Deal with suppliers on line	Faster and cheaper than telephone and post	1
Advertise our services	We want more business	Put details and prices on line	Pro: millions of users Con: hit and miss	3
Get feedback on our products	We want to improve the quality	Use online forms	Easier than writing a letter	2

Summary

Spend time thinking before you write.

Talk to other people to help you sort out your ideas.

Ask yourself what your site is for.

Test your ideas against a list of possibilities.

Be clear in your mind what your site is not for: avoid setting up false expectations.

Answer the question 'What does it do?' in ten words.

Who is it for?

It takes two to communicate

In this chapter, we deal with the second question you should ask yourself before you write anything: Who is it for? There are two exercises to help you establish the kind of words that will most effectively connect with your target user.

Once you've decided what you want your site to do, you need to think who it will do it for. It is meant to be useful. Who is going to use it? People you know, people in your neighbourhood, people all over the country, people anywhere in the world? What sort of person – young, artistic, pensioner, female, educated, self-employed, male, business, professional, student? Who are you aiming at?

It takes two to communicate

Writing involves two people, not just one. It is not enough to put an idea into words. You have to be sure that the idea is received by the other person as you intended. It has to evoke the appropriate response. The bulb has to light up, so to speak. In certain kinds of communication, there are formulae for expressing this. On a ship, the traditional response to an order is 'Aye, aye, sir'. Over the radio, it goes one step further with 'Message received and understood'.

As the Web is an interactive medium, it is important to think about the person on the receiving end and how your writing can get the response you hope for. If you want a person to do something as a result of what you write – buy something, write back or tell someone else – try asking yourself 'What would persuade me to do it?' or 'How would I react to this?' Read out what you have written to someone else and see how they react.

In Chapter 1, I asked you to put yourself in the position of the user and compare the way we use books or listen to radio with the way we use websites. That's where you should be as much as possible, looking at the site through the user's eyes. The way you write depends on who you think is going to find your site useful.

Try it yourself. Take a simple story, for example what you did yesterday, and write two versions of it. Write four sentences to an eight-year-old boy you know and four to a senior figure in your own or some other organisation. Compare the words you use in the two versions. In the case of the child, your purpose is clear: your whole attention is focused on making it easy for him to understand. In the other case, your language is likely to become pompous and the words long. Your purpose is confused: you want to inform, but you also want to impress (Table 3.1).

Table 3.1 Write two versions of a simple story.

To an eight-year-old boy	To a senior person
I went with some friends from the office to see a play. It was all about a family that was very unhappy. The Mum and Dad and two boys seemed to hate each other and each told awful stories about how bad the others were. We were tired and a bit sad by the end, so we had a pizza to cheer ourselves up before going home.	I took some colleagues to see Long Day's Journey into Night. Long it certainly was! Who ever imagined that dysfunctional families and drug addiction were modern phenomena? It was brilliantly performed, but a somewhat cathartic experience requiring remedial quantities of refreshment afterwards.

One of the best bits of advice on this aspect of writing appears in the preface to the *Plain English Handbook* put out by the Securities and Exchange Commission (SEC) in the United States. It is written by the investment expert Warren Buffett, whose company is called Berkshire Hathaway. He says:

> Write with a specific person in mind. When writing Berkshire Hathaway's annual report, I pretend that I'm talking to my sisters. I have no trouble picturing them: though highly intelligent, they are not experts in accounting or finance. They will understand plain English, but jargon may puzzle them. My goal is simply to give them the information I would wish them to supply me if our positions were reversed. To succeed, I don't need to be Shakespeare; I must, though, have a sincere desire to inform. No siblings to write to? Borrow mine: just begin with 'Dear Doris and Bertie'.

What's wrong with jargon? Jargon is a kind of shorthand used by colleagues at work or people engaged in the same activity. It facilitates communication within a group and fosters a sense of belonging. So it may be fine to use jargon if you know that the person you are addressing is one of the group. The problem arises when you are trying to communicate with someone who is not, as in Buffett's example. The SEC's plain English campaign is based on the premise that you should not need to be an insider to understand a company report or share offer. It is in a company's interest to communicate successfully with investors, and investors need to understand the documents if they are to make informed decisions.

One way of making yourself more sensitive to jargon is to practise drawing up lists of in-words for different groups of people – computer buffs, sportspeople, musicians, car enthusiasts, gardeners, accountants and so on (Table 3.2). Look at the lists and decide which words are suitable for the people you are aiming at and which are not. If your site is for people working in a particular field or with a particular interest, the in-words or jargon may help create a sense of community. If your site is not for specialists, one or two in-words may still help establish your credibility. Up to a point, you can carry people with you – they may even be interested in finding out about a word they don't understand – but you have to judge at what point you will lose them.

Table 3.2 Drawing up a list of in-words.

Accountants' jargon	
Asset turnover	
Buffer budgets	
Consistency	
Contribution	
Depreciation	
Gearing	
Liabilities	
Matching	
Opportunity cost	
Realisation	
Relevant cost	
SWOT analysis	

What matters is that you keep the user in mind. Your website should be designed from the user's point of view and what they can get out of it, rather than from your point of view and what you want to say. Too many sites, especially organisations' first attempts at putting themselves on line, start by saying, in effect, 'Here we are. This is our mission statement, here's a photograph of our chairman and that building is our new headquarters.' Who cares? The first question a user asks of a website is 'What will it do for me?'

As a Web writer, your task is to answer that question, then to try answer the questions you think the user will ask, in the order you think they will ask them. But the Web is non-linear. The fact that there is no set order makes it even more important to think through your information and organise it well.

Summary

Writing involves two people, not one.

Your purpose is to get a response from another person.

Choose your words with that person and that purpose in mind.

Answer the user's first question: 'What will this site do for me?'

All through the site, write with the user's needs in mind.

What's the story?

4

What is it about? This chapter gives you advice on how to organise the information in your site.

Every website tells a story. In fact it must tell several stories according to the questions the user asks of it. The user will decide what line to take from the information that you offer. The variations are huge. Now that you have clearly defined your purpose and decided who you hope will use your site, you need to work out what the likely questions are and how you are going to answer them. That means organising your information.

The starting point

Imagine a user arriving at your home page. What do they need to know? Answer: what the site offers. The user will probably decide in a couple of seconds whether the site is interesting or not. That decision will be influenced by the colour and the layout of the page, and the speed at which it loads, but research suggests that what the user looks for is words. The words on your home page need to convey an idea and explain it simply. They must welcome and engage the user, as economically as possible.

It's tempting to put as much on the home page as you can, to show off everything you've got, but it's usually a mistake. The user can't take it in, and you can't afford to confuse or mislead, or they'll go elsewhere. The task is to think hard about what makes your site special and to describe it, not with hyperbole but precisely and in as few words as possible. The question you are asking yourself is 'What is the least the user needs to know to want to go further into my site?' You will probably spend hours, even days, trying to get the words right.

You can read about the home page in more detail in Chapter 12. At this stage, if you are clear about the central idea of your site, you can spend some time working out what information you need to put on your site and how to plan it. You might try using a Mind Map®.

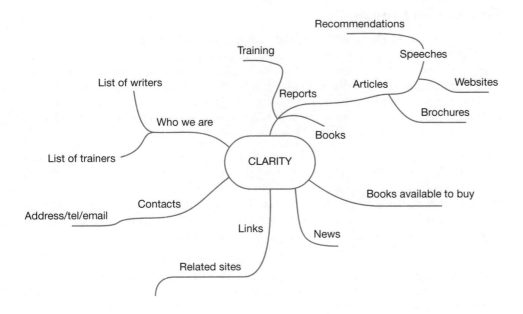

Figure 4.1 Using a Mind Map® to plan your site.

Generating ideas

Take a sheet of A4 paper and write the central idea of your site in the middle. It may be an event, the unique service you are offering or just the name of your company. Then put yourself in the position of the person who is going to use the site. Think what this person is likely to want from you and write down ideas as they occur to you, along lines branching out from the central idea. Some will follow on from one another, some will form a new branch from the central idea. When you run out of ideas, stand back and have a look (Figure 4.1).

Unlike traditional linear notes, the Mind Map® allows you to see all your ideas at once. Unlike linear notes, it mirrors our natural pattern of thinking, which is by association. Best of all, it works in a similar way to the Web, because of the unique feature of the Web – the link. The link enables you to follow the natural pattern of thinking, so that in the ideal site, when an idea occurs to you you can follow it by a link. This is what you are aiming for.

If you are working in a group and have access to a whiteboard, so much the better. Then you can brainstorm as a group. The first phase of brainstorming is for generating ideas. Let everyone call out ideas with one person writing them down. Every idea, however off-the-wall, is noted. No one should question or contradict them at this stage: it's a time for ideas to flow freely. Then you can go through the ideas together, pull them apart, discuss them and agree which to discard and which to keep. The third phase is for putting them back together in a structured way (Table 4.1).

A whiteboard is useful because it allows you to move ideas around, take them out and put them back, or rewrite them. If you don't have a whiteboard, you may like to use a conventional board with sticky bits of paper. Write each idea on a separate bit of paper and stick it on the board. Then as you discuss the

Table 4.1 Brainstorming.

Phase	Activity	Time allowed
Creative	Everyone calls out ideas as they occur. One person writes them all down.	10%
Analytical	Go through the ideas together. Discuss the pros and cons of each. Agree which to discard.	60%
Organisational	Decide which ideas belong together and put them into groups. Label each group.	30%

ideas, you can move the bits of paper around, discard them or put them back and finally put them in groups. Bits of ordinary paper on a table or on the floor will do, but pieces of card work better as they are less likely to fly away and are easier to move around on a table or carpet.

Putting them together

When you are organising, you need to be rigorous. You can do such a lot on the Web. You can find Einstein's essay on relativity, or look at a facsimile of a medieval manuscript, as easily as you can read a bus timetable or tomorrow's weather forecast. It's tempting to think of all the things you can do, rather than concentrating on the least you need to do to make the site work. Think back all the time to what the site is for and reject anything that is not essential to your purpose. This will make your task much easier.

Organising your material into categories is like creating a filing system. Think how difficult it can be to find things in other people's files, or in unfamiliar supermarkets, and remember: this is for someone else to use.

The most familiar ways of organising information are alphabetically and chronologically. Users will quickly understand a system organised in either of these ways and feel comfortable looking for things in it, but these systems work best when people know what they are looking for and there is only one right answer. Looking for someone's telephone number in a directory is easy as long as you know their full name and probably their address. To find an article in a newspaper archive that is organised chronologically you need to know the date of publication. Even geographical organisation, although familiar, requires some knowledge on the part of the user. Most website users don't know exactly what they want: they come to a site with a general question, a vague idea of what they want, and expect to be offered solutions and to learn things.

Most websites are organised in a more subjective way – by topic, function or user group, or a mixture of systems. Yellow Pages are an example of information organised by topic and then put in alphabetical order, and many websites are similarly organised into categories of products or services. Other sites are organised by function, according to what users might want out of the site – to browse, to buy, to find a local dealer or find out more about the company

(Figure 4.2). If organising by user group is more suitable for your site, you will think of your likely users and put them into categories, as for example a company might divide potential clients into corporate and individual, while also offering categories of news likely to be of interest to all users (Figure 4.3).

Figure 4.2 Organising a website by function.

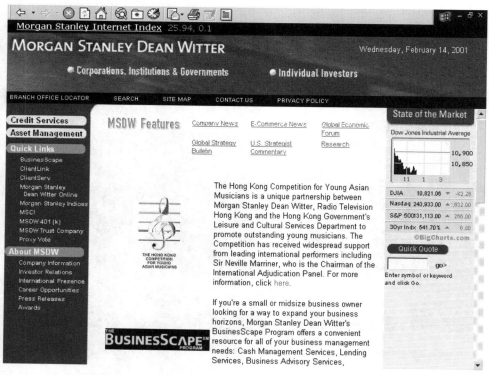

Figure 4.3 Organising a website by user group.

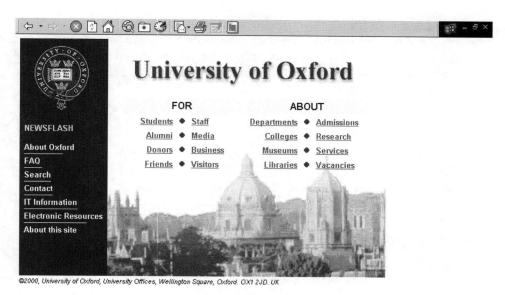

©2000, University of Oxford, University Offices, Wellington Square, Oxford. OX1 2JD. UK

Figure 4.4 Using two ways of organising information.

If, for example, you organise your information by both user group and topic, a mixture of systems enables you to present the user with a lot of options immediately (Figure 4.4).

The hierarchy

At this point you need to think about the hierarchy of information. This may sound like a contradiction of what we've said about the Web being non-linear and using Mind Maps® instead of linear notes, but one of the key considerations in organising a website is how quickly the user can get what they want. Many sites are based on the principle that the user should be able to find what they are looking for in no more than, say, three clicks. So you need to decide on levels of information in the order you think the user will respond to what you tell them on the home page (Figure 4.5).

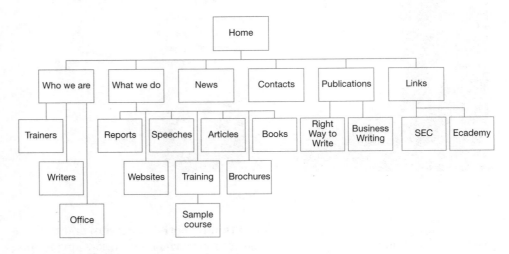

Figure 4.5 Hierarchy of information on a website.

For example, on a site selling widgets, the user will want to know very soon how much they cost and how to get them. Who makes them is of little interest if they are made in a factory. If, on the other hand, they are individually made in some traditional way, the personality of the craftsman may be a selling point and should be high up the hierarchy. If your site is offering a service, the qualifications of the people providing it are important; the cost may be less of a consideration. If your site is about an event, then how to get there is one of the first things the user will want to know; and so on.

Practise a number of story lines. Imagine a particular user, create a character and a scenario for them, then test your organisation of the information so far to see how well it works.

On a website, again because you want information to be accessible in the fewest number of clicks, the hierarchy should be broad and shallow rather than narrow and deep. Aim for between three and seven categories. Fewer than three isn't a list; more than seven items is hard to take in. If you find your list of options getting longer than seven, either divide the options again or arrange them in a way that quickly becomes obvious, such as alphabetical order.

Chunks and links

The chunks of information should be discrete, i.e. they should make sense on their own and the same information should not appear in different places. To make the organisation easier for the user to understand, each chunk should tell a separate story. The great thing about the Web is that having arranged your information in a hierarchy, you can still have a link straight from level 2 to something on level 4. You can, for example, offer the user the chance to go straight to buying a widget or the opportunity to find out more about it before deciding. There can be two or more ways of getting to the same chunk. Also, saying that the same information should not appear in different places does not mean you do not repeat key ideas. On the contrary, the name of your site and what makes it special should appear often to reinforce your message and maintain the identity of the site.

You have divided your information into chunks and made sure that each says something distinct. You have determined their relationship to one another, which is mostly hierarchical, but with some direct links. Now you need to think how you are going to link them in your writing. As you write the text on one page, you need to be thinking where the user might want to go next. If, for example, you are describing a conference and you have a particularly interesting speaker, you not only put a link to the speaker on that page, you mention the person in the text so that the user is encouraged to use the link.

Even if you don't design it yourself, understanding the structure of the site will help your writing. Realising what it's like to come to a site without any idea of what is in it makes you think how you can explain the site to the user. Knowing what is in it makes you write your text with the possible links in mind and makes the site both richer and more coherent.

Summary

Make sure your website tells a story, in fact several different stories.

Sum up what you are offering in a few words.

Try to describe the content on a single piece of paper.

Be rigorous when deciding what your site will do. A focused site will work better.

Organise your information into chunks.

Plan your hierarchy.

Make the hierarchy as shallow as possible.

Think how you are going to link the information.

Test your plan by imagining a user going through your site in several different ways.

Be aware of the structure of your site when you write.

The language of the Web

Inclusive writing

Appropriate writing

Conversational writing

Polished writing

This chapter talks about good writing in any context as writing which does its job. It looks at the differences between written and spoken English and where the Web fits in. It briefly discusses style.

Good writing is writing that does its job. It achieves its purpose, whether that is to tell you how to operate a lawn mower, to persuade you to book a holiday or to move you to tears over the suffering of a person you don't even know. On a website, we are mainly concerned with the first two types of writing rather than the third. The point of mentioning the third is to stress that writing is always functional.

Language is a tool. Its function is to enable people to deal with one another. Just as it can reinforce a sense of community, it can also be used to enable some people to communicate at the expense of others. Children do it all the time. They invent languages to draw a boundary between themselves and grown-ups or other children. Groups in society use words to draw boundaries between themselves and others. They recognise certain words as defining the class or group a person belongs to. If you use these words, you're in; if you use those words, you're out. As soon as the in-words are taken up by the outsiders, the code is changed, for the purpose of the in-language is not to communicate with outsiders but to exclude them.

Inclusive writing

On the Web, you don't want to use a special language that only a few people can understand, nor is it a good idea to use words in a way that is peculiar to your site. There are already plenty of new words that people have had to learn in order to use the Web. For most websites, you want to write in a way that as many people as possible will understand. In any context, good writing is writing that is immediately understandable. It should not need to be read more than once. On the Web, a highly competitive environment where users spend money to be on line, poor writing may simply mean the end of the communication. The user gives up and goes elsewhere.

There has been a rapid convergence of terminology on the Web as the number of users has grown. In the early days every site was different; every site had its own navigation, almost its own language. There were relatively few sites. Users had to be technically competent to be there at all and they were prepared to work at understanding each site. No more. With millions of sites and anyone expecting to be able to use them, users are not going to bother with a site that does not explain itself well and uses words differently from other sites.

Appropriate writing

If you have bought anything from the bookseller Amazon, you may have noticed that amazon.com uses an American term 'shopping cart' (Figure 5.1), whereas amazon.co.uk uses the more British 'shopping basket' (Figure 5.2). If you thought that 'shopping bag' might be more appropriate for your customers, you would have to weigh up the value of making your site appear more upmarket against the potential loss of customers who didn't recognise 'bag' as having the same function as 'basket'. In a very short time, shoppers on the Web have got used to terms such as 'shopping basket'. They expect sites with similar functions to use similar words.

There is nothing new in this. Compare the Bible and Shakespeare. The King James Bible uses about half the number of words in an educated person's vocabulary. Shakespeare, on the other hand, is reckoned to have had twice the educated person's vocabulary. Shakespeare's plays and the King James Bible were both written at a time of extraordinary growth in the English language, yet one used nearly four times as many different words as the other.

This is because their functions were quite different. The Bible was for instruction. It was intended to be understood and learned by as many people as possible. Repetition of a relatively small number of words suited its purpose. Shakespeare's purpose, on the other hand, was to stimulate the imagination; to conjure up scenes and characters in different periods of history and different countries, real and imagined. He used dozens of new words, and as many as he could, to fulfil his purpose. It didn't matter that not everyone understood every word.

In the number of words it uses, the Web is at the Bible's end of the spectrum, rather than Shakespeare's. Restricting the vocabulary makes the medium easy to operate.

Conversational writing

What kinds of words should the Web use? Remember that the Web was set up to share things. As well as enabling us to share information, it allows us to do business, pursue common interests and create communities. Communication on the Web is immediate. It works best when it is informal and individual. Because the Web is interactive, because it allows conversations that are almost real, its language should be conversational. The site should 'speak' to the user in a welcoming and friendly, but efficient, way. The conversation, however, is not real. Think of all the jokes and sad stories about people who 'met' on the Internet and then met in reality. Think of all the misunderstandings and even

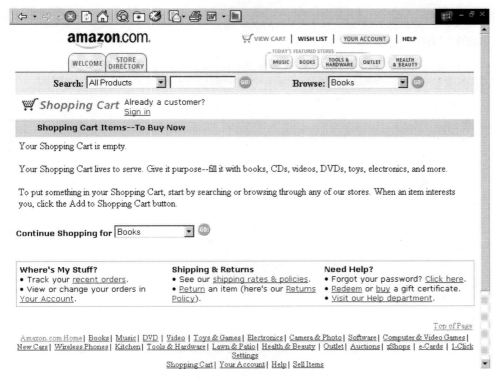

Figure 5.1 The shopping cart at amazon.com.

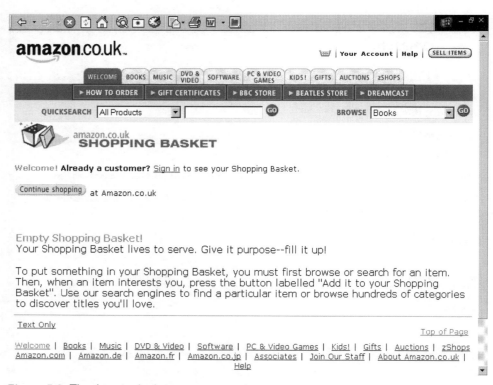

Figure 5.2 The shopping basket at amazon.co.uk.

crises within an organisation caused by emails. That's because people write as if they are having a conversation and forget that the vital ingredient of a conversation – the other person – is missing.

This is the crucial difference between written and spoken English. When we have a conversation with someone, we are far more influenced by their physical appearance, their facial expression, attitude and the way they move, their tone of voice and manner of speaking, than we are by the words they use. The words themselves account for about 10% of the communication between us. Try it yourself. How do you feel if someone says she really cares about you, while staring through the window at something going on outside? Imagine seeing television pictures of a man shaking his fists and looking furious, with a commentary saying 'Henry has just completed a course in meditation'. Which do you believe, what you see or what you hear?

There was a striking example of the power of visual information in the 1960 US presidential election. The candidates, Richard Nixon and John Kennedy, debated the issues on television. Their speeches were also broadcast on the radio. Afterwards the audiences were asked which candidate had won the debate. The radio listeners gave it to Nixon, the television viewers to Kennedy. The television viewers were apparently swayed by Kennedy's clean good looks compared with Nixon's sweaty unshaven face. Kennedy looked confident, Nixon looked shifty. The words were overpowered.

The way we speak conveys an enormous amount of meaning. Think of how many different ways you can say a simple phrase like 'You know'. Depending on the context, your attitude, your gestures, tone of voice and volume, you can make those words a statement of fact, a question, a threat, a declaration of love, an exclamation of astonishment, the punchline of a joke and so on. If you describe someone as 'quite reliable', you can by your tone of voice say either that the person is reliable or that he is not. Without the physical presence of the speaker, words have to work hard to convey meaning accurately.

Without the physical presence of the other person, the listener or reader, communication can easily go awry. If you tell a joke and no one laughs, you get your feedback straight away – it fell flat. When you speak to someone, you soon know whether you are retaining their interest, or whether your message is getting through as intended. If they look bored or puzzled you can change pace, change the subject, ask them a question or try it again a different way. When you write, none of these options is open to you. The words have to do it all.

A halfway house between speaking to someone in person and writing to them is talking on the telephone. You have the tone of voice and the possibility of immediate reaction to help the conversation. Indeed, the fact that the other person is not in front of you may sometimes make the conversation easier than it would be in person. The telephone conversation can be the most intimate form of communication. This is where unthinking emailers often make their mistake. They confuse the email with a telephone conversation and write as if they were talking to the other person. They have no way of knowing what mood the recipient is in, get no immediate reaction and have no opportunity to clarify any misunderstanding.

There are conventions about what we can and cannot say in writing. For example, it is said that a contraction like 'couldn't', which is normal in speech, should always be replaced by 'could not' in writing. Some publications follow that rule, others don't. This Simple Guide uses contractions, except where the full words provide the right emphasis, in order to sound conversational. Any such convention is, or should be, designed to help your written English make up for the 90% of communication that is missing when the person you are communicating with is not there.

Your Web writing should sound conversational. Even though it is not intended to be read aloud, it should also sound good. You will choose one word rather than another because it sounds better as you read it to yourself. You may write 'jail' rather than 'prison', not because of any difference in meaning between the two words but because one syllable suits the rhythm of the sentence better than two. One reason great literature is great is that it was mostly written to be read aloud. One reason bad writing is bad is that the writer hasn't bothered to listen to it.

Polished writing

While the tone of your words should be like a conversation, the text that appears on a website must look as good as in a magazine. This makes writing for the Web very demanding. You are writing as if in a conversation, but without the other person. In your thinking and planning, you are trying to anticipate the user's reactions to what you say. At the same time you are writing as if for a magazine. Your words may be on the screen for a few minutes before you rewrite them or they may be printed out and kept for weeks. Either way, they must look good. The speed with which people expect to get what they want from a website means the language must be clear and direct. The speed with which they may move from one page to another places a premium on consistency of style and usage.

Before I go on to help you meet these demands, we need to deal with the question of style. You may be wondering what style of writing you ought to adopt for the Web. Don't – or at least don't spend time worrying about it. If you adopt a style that does not come easily to you, you are unlikely to write well. If you are concerned about how you are coming across, you are unlikely to come across well. If you are thinking about yourself, rather than the person you are writing for and what you are writing about, you are putting an obstacle in the way of your purpose in writing. The Victorian poet Matthew Arnold had this reassurance for writers:

> People think I can teach them style. What stuff it all is! Have something to say, and say it as clearly as you can. That is the only secret of style.

Summary

Writing is always functional: the language you use depends on your purpose.

On the Web, you usually want to communicate with as many people as possible.

It helps if you limit and standardise your vocabulary.

Web writing should be conversational.

The words have to work hard because the other person is not there.

The writing must sound good and look good.

Your purpose will determine your style.

Using as few words as possible

6

Have you thought it through?

Are you sure what that word means?

Is that word necessary?

Is there a simpler way of saying it?

Are you really trying to inform?

The first rule of Web writing is to be concise. Here are some questions and guidelines to help you use as few words as possible, with exercises for you to practise on.

Every word on a website must justify itself. The space on a screen is limited, you have very little time to get your message across and the user is impatient. Your aim should be to use as few words as possible.

Have you thought it through?

One reason people use too many words is that they haven't really thought about what they want to say. So they waffle. Thinking about the three questions: Why am I writing? For whom? About what? will help you avoid over-writing. We discussed the purpose of your writing in Chapter 2 and the person you are writing for in Chapter 3. We'll now deal with the third element – the subject matter.

Think of all the times you have had to read something several times to understand it, or perhaps never to understand it at all. The chances are that the writer didn't fully understand it either. You can't hope to put information across to someone else if you haven't digested it yourself. Think of the occasions you have found something difficult to write. The chances are that your source material was hard to understand or there was some information missing or you just hadn't done enough work on it. Consciously or unconsciously, you are not happy writing about something you don't fully understand yourself. Once your thoughts are clear, you can set about choosing the words that express them accurately.

Are you sure what that word means?

Another reason people use too many words is that they are not sure of their meaning. It's a good idea to keep a dictionary by your side and check that words mean what you think they do. Using words precisely is like having a range of sharp tools at your disposal. Not only are they sharp but each is appropriate to a particular purpose. You would not have much confidence in a plumber who told you he had one or two tools that did all right for most jobs. Too often we rely on a few expressions to cover most eventualities and end up describing none of them effectively.

In his play *The Real Thing*, Tom Stoppard likens good writing to making a cricket bat:

> This thing here, which looks like a wooden club, is actually several pieces of particular wood cunningly put together in a certain way so that the whole thing is sprung, like a dance floor. It's for hitting cricket balls with. If you get it right, the cricket ball will travel two hundred yards in four seconds ... What we're trying to do is to write cricket bats, so that when we throw up an idea and give it a little knock, it might travel.

The same character goes on to describe words as:

> ... innocent, neutral, precise, standing for this, describing that, meaning the other, so if you look after them you can build bridges across incomprehension and chaos. But when they get their corners knocked off, they're no good any more ...

The meanings of words change. New words are introduced into the language all the time. In order to understand one another, we have to agree about the meaning of words. This is more, not less, vital in a medium that works so quickly, where people expect the message to be immediately clear, otherwise they are off. You can't afford to be a Humpty Dumpty. 'When I use a word,' Humpty Dumpty said, in a rather scornful tone, 'it means just what I choose it to mean – neither more nor less' (*Through the Looking-Glass*, Lewis Carroll). You need to look around you all the time and be aware of how other sites are using words. When it comes to the essential functions of your site, conformity is a virtue.

Is that word necessary?

After laziness in preparation comes laziness in writing. We are all guilty of tautology, saying the same thing twice, and of using unnecessary words (Tables 6.1 and 6.2). We talk of a 'serious crisis' as though there might be one that didn't matter, or a 'rather unique' occasion as though there were shades of uniqueness. When writing, we need to go through the words we have chosen to make sure every one is needed. The following passage contains many words whose meaning is already expressed by other words or phrases. Practise cutting text by crossing out unnecessary words. You should be able to get rid of at least 20 (see page 53).

Setting up your website involves co-operative collaboration between the various members of a team, such as the designer and the commissioner, for example. The method is a simple one.

Pre-planning is an essential requirement. A practical manual is a helpful support and meeting on a daily or weekly basis is also good practice. Only one person should be in charge, but each member of the team, however, must necessarily be kept informed at every single stage of the project. If not, it can otherwise completely break down.

Undue haste in launching your website should be strongly resisted. Seeing the empty space where your website should be may tend to lead to anxious concern. That is as nothing compared with the horrific nightmare of a website that does not work well.

Table 6.1 Tautology.

free gift	the reason is because
top priority	successfully refute
pre-condition	knock-on effect
past history	undue haste
future prospects	careful consideration
no other alternative	real danger
we are all unanimous	attempt to try

Table 6.2 One word will do.

divide up	
head up	
meet up with	
merge together	
thinking mentally	
overall picture	
crisis situation	
ongoing plan	
test out	

Is there a simpler way of saying it?

A fourth reason for verbosity is that people use a phrase rather than a single word to say what they mean. Why use the phrase 'make adjustments to' when you can use one word, 'adjust'? It's almost as if people are frightened of the true meaning of words. Perhaps asking someone to 'co-ordinate arrangements for a party' does make the task sound less daunting than 'arranging' it, but there is no difference in meaning. Certainly politicians and others use language to avoid confronting reality, and we come back to that in Chapters 7 and 8, but on a website you are trying to communicate clearly and concisely. You may like to practise finding a single word that conveys the same meaning as commonly used phrases.

> We *have absolute confidence in our ability to* deliver this by Monday.

> He *came to a decision* to buy the shares.

> I am writing to you *with regard to* your proposal.

> He was unable to be at the wedding *owing to the fact that* he had broken his leg.

Are you really trying to inform?

A fifth reason for verbosity is the desire to impress (again). We seem to think it's rude to write briefly, as though words are presents and our reader deserves lots of them. More likely we think that a long letter, report or article shows how much effort we have put in. The opposite is true. It takes far more effort to write concisely, because you have to think and plan, and choose and edit your words. Why should your reader have to wade through three times as many words as necessary? Blaise Pascal, the French philosopher, acknowledged the selfishness of long-winded writers when he ended a letter to a friend: 'I am sorry this is such a long letter. I did not have time to write a short one.'

Table 6.3 Prefer a single word to a phrase.

Phrase	Word
make an application	apply
give an undertaking	undertake
make use of	use
serves to explain	explains
in respect of	for
in the vicinity of	near
in the event that	if
despite the fact that	although
with the result that	and

Using few words may sometimes seem abrupt, but if they are the right ones, how powerful they can be! When the Quaker William Penn was arrested for addressing a meeting in the street in 1670, he wrote to his dying father from prison. He began his letter 'Because I cannot come, I write'. In our century, think how long a company takes, and how much money it spends, to come up with an advertising slogan of perhaps three words. Those three words may be worth millions of pounds.

Is every word working?

When you are trying to write concisely, there is a journalist's device called the Fish Shop Test you can use to remind you to pare your text to the minimum. Imagine going to a fish shop. There are fish laid out on the slab in the window. On the window is a notice, 'Fresh Fish Sold Here'. What information does it give you? None that you do not already have. You wouldn't expect the fishmonger to be in business if he was selling stale fish. So you can get rid of 'Fresh'. You can see the 'Fish' in the window so you know that's what his business is. He's certainly not giving it away, so you don't need 'Sold', or 'Here' because it is obviously a fish shop.

Every word has to justify itself. Some Web guides argue that putting 'click here' on a Web page is like putting a notice on a shop door saying 'Depress handle, push door and walk in'. That may be going a bit far when you think how many people are still finding their way around the Web. But it is good practice to test every word you use, to make sure it is adding value, not saying something that is already obvious. For the fishmonger, this might have been 'Welcome' or 'Lobsters every Thursday in June'.

A shop is a good metaphor for a website, so here's another shop example. There's a hardware shop in Woodstock in Oxfordshire that has a notice above the door saying 'Service with a snarl'. It's a useful shop, the owner is helpful and you nearly always find what you are looking for. So the shop does what you expect, but the notice is intriguing. It makes you look twice at the shop and remember it. That is using words to add value.

Table 6.4 Without the unnecessary words.

Setting up your website involves collaboration between the members of a team, such as the designer and the commissioner. The method is simple.

Planning is essential. A manual is helpful and meeting daily or weekly is also good practice. One person should be in charge, but each member of the team must be kept informed at every stage of the project. If not, it can break down.

Haste in launching your website should be resisted. Seeing the space where your website should be may lead to concern. That is nothing compared with the nightmare of a website that does not work.

Summary

Before you write, think what you want to say.

Be sure you understand what you are writing about.

Choose your words carefully.

Make sure they mean what you think they do.

Use words that everyone will understand.

Use a single word rather than a phrase.

Check that every word is working.

Choosing the right words

What to avoid

How to make bad writing better

This chapter starts with the kinds of words you should avoid if you want to be clear and concise. Then it looks at the kinds of words you should be using. There are examples of bad writing, with exercises showing how to improve it.

What to avoid

Jargon and slang

Avoid jargon because it excludes. As we said in Chapter 3, jargon is a language for insiders. It has a useful function within a group or an organisation as a kind of shorthand that enables people to communicate easily about what they are doing, but it can also be used to show off knowledge, wealth or social standing for the sole purpose of making the other person feel inferior. If you want to communicate with as many people as possible, don't use it.

Avoid slang for the same reasons. You can't be sure that everyone you want to reach will understand 'wicked' to mean the same as you do or that they will understand words such as 'diss' at all. Slang is mostly used by people who know one another, who share the same culture and are of the same age group. Again, unless you are sure that you want to communicate exclusively with those people, avoid it.

Terms that exclude

Words that may not constitute jargon or slang may still be exclusive. In order to communicate we have to assume some common points of reference, but we can take this too far. A website that asks you for your zip code assumes it is talking to people in the United States. It makes people outside the United States feel it is not meant for them, even though they might be interested in the content.

Since one of the strengths of the Web is that it can bring people together regardless of where they are, it makes sense to try to make the language we use as inclusive as possible. Even within one country, we make a lot of assumptions about shared experiences and values. A forecast of rain may be welcome to farmers and unwelcome to holidaymakers. People don't all know the same music, read the same books, watch the same television programmes or do the same things to amuse themselves on a Sunday; and this sentence makes several cultural assumptions, including the assumption that everyone takes Sunday off. It comes down to thinking about all the people who might use your site and choosing the appropriate words.

Cliches

The next type of words to avoid is cliches. Cliches are yesterday's inspirations. The phrase 'over the moon' is wonderfully expressive of joy. It conjures up a picture of the cow jumping over the moon in the nursery rhyme *Hey Diddle Diddle*. The first time it was used it must have been very effective. The hundred-and-first time, it doesn't impress. It suggests that the person who uses it has not thought, has not chosen his words himself but has pulled something ready-made off the shelf. The writer George Orwell described hackneyed prose as consisting 'less of words chosen for the sake of their meaning, and more ... of phrases tacked together like the sections of a pre-fabricated hen-house'.

Metaphors such as 'over the moon' and similes such as 'like the sections of a pre-fabricated hen-house' communicate an idea by creating a picture in the reader's mind. But whereas the hen-house is original, 'over the moon' is not. If every word on a website is to justify itself, it should be individually chosen to do its job. George Orwell died long before websites were invented, but as the greatest exponent of clear, simple English in the past century he still has a lot to say about good writing in any medium.

Long, pompous words

The English language is so rich in words that you often have a choice between a short, pithy word and a long, cumbersome one that means the same. The short, pithy one will usually be of German origin, having come into English via the Anglo-Saxons or Danes, and the long, cumbersome one will usually have come from Latin, thanks mainly to the Christian church and the French spoken by the Norman kings and barons (Table 7.1). You can guess why people choose the long words. Latin was for so long the language of the educated and the powerful and the habit dies hard. We still, subconsciously even, want to show that we can talk like the elite.

Table 7.1 We often have a choice of words that mean the same.

Latin origin	German origin
currently	now
purchase	buy
disadvantage	drawback
respond to	answer
facilitate	make easy
illumination	light
assistance	help
inform	tell
install	put
prior to	before
discontinue	stop
requirements	needs

Having in effect two vocabularies provides not just synonyms but also many shades of meaning. We use the Anglo-Saxon or Old English word 'read' in the same way as speakers of Latin languages use derivations of 'legere', from which we get 'legible'. Yet readable and legible mean different things. To say text is readable means it is easy and enjoyable to read; to say it is legible just means it can be read.

On top of those two sets of words are the words we have adopted and continue to adopt from Greek, often in technical and scientific language, such as 'micro' and 'macro', and the thousands of words we have adopted from languages all over the world.

Whatever their origin, the test for the words on your website is whether they work. Look at how 'extensive' is used on the site in Figure 7.1. An index of previous articles is a good way of making use of old material on a website, and printing it off is the easiest way of reading it, but 'extensive' was not a strong enough word to prevent me starting to read the list on screen, scrolling down and getting entangled and then cross. The warning was there, but you can't rely on the user reading every word, and 'extensive' failed to do its job. 'Very long' might have had more effect.

Negative expressions
Avoiding negative expressions doesn't mean saying something is good when it's bad. It means expressing your ideas in a positive way. Ideas that are expressed positively are easier to understand (Table 7.2). If you say you are 'not proud' of something you have done, the listener has to conjure up two ideas in quick succession – what it means to be proud and that you are not whatever it is. If instead you say you 'regret' it, the listener has only one idea to grasp. Ideas that

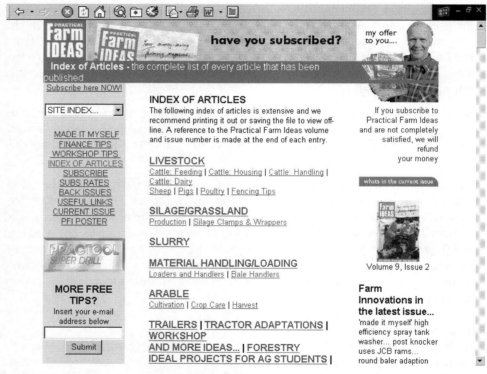

Figure 7.1 Note the use of the word 'extensive'.

are expressed positively are also likely to be more definite than those expressed negatively. If you say 'I wasn't annoyed', it begs the question 'What you did feel?' Saying one thing is 'not unlike' another requires the listener to do mental gymnastics and still leaves him with only a vague idea of what you mean.

Table 7.2 Expressing ideas positively.

Negative	Positive
Does not include	Leaves out
Not unless	Only if
Not often	Rarely
Don't use	Avoid using
Does not have	Lacks
Not many	Few
Don't ignore	Listen to
Non-members will not receive invitations	Only members will be invited

So far this chapter has been about what to avoid. That may itself seem negative, but 'avoid' is a positive way of saying 'don't use'. Besides, advice is often best understood by seeing what happens when you ignore it. We learn more from mistakes than successes and rules are nearly always drawn up as a result of things going wrong. You may know a website called WebPagesThatSuck.com, which aims to help people learn how to design websites by showing them examples of bad design.

How to make bad writing better

Now to what you should be doing. How do you improve a really bad piece of writing? You can cross out unnecessary words, you can replace phrases with single words and you can replace long Latinate words with short Germanic ones. But you can only go so far. You may still have a bad bit of prose. To rewrite it radically, you have to look at the structure of the language. Start with an example of office verbosity:

> The position in regard to office accommodation at the present time is characterised by a shortfall of four hundred square metres in terms of the need versus availability. The space situation requires review on a monthly basis. An immediate solution is not a practicable proposition, but we have absolute confidence in the ability of the facilities department to maximise their efforts and it is envisaged that an overall solution will materialise in the short- to medium term.

You can change 'at the present time' to 'now' and replace 'maximise their efforts' with 'try hard'. You know that 'short- to medium term' is meaningless unless you have a timetable, so you can put 'soon' instead. But the problem is not just in the particular words chosen: it is in the kinds of words they are. To make it better, you need to read the piece through, work out what the writer is trying to say, and express those ideas differently. It could go something like this:

> We are four hundred square metres short of office space. We need to review the position every month. There is no immediate solution, but the facilities department are doing their best and we are sure they will come up with something soon.

What did we do? First we put in a personal pronoun, 'we'. This is a message from a manager to staff about something that affects them directly. It should be written in a personal way, from me to you, not impersonally as if it were a description of something happening elsewhere (Table 7.3).

Table 7.3 Expressing yourself in a personal way.

Impersonal/noun	Personal/verb
A fault has become apparent	I have made a mistake
A preferential rate is not an option	We cannot offer you a preferential rate
In the event of an accident occurring	If you have an accident
It is not our wish to be impersonal	We do not wish to seem impersonal
Your disappointment is apparent	You are obviously disappointed

Change the construction

By starting the first sentence with 'We', you change the construction of the sentence. Instead of an impersonal, passive construction, 'The position is characterised by a shortfall of ...', you have a personal, active one, 'We are ... short.' That allows you to get rid of the vague words and phrases such as 'The position in regard to', 'is characterised by', 'a shortfall of' and 'in terms of the need versus availability'.

The same with the second sentence. Replace a passive construction, 'The space situation requires review', with an active one, 'We need to review'. Not only have you shortened it, you have included more information: you have said who needs to do the review. One reason the passive voice is used so often is that it is a way of avoiding responsibility. 'It is envisaged that an overall solution …' in the third sentence does just that. It appears to give the staff information, but unless they know who to go back to when the problem is not solved, it is useless.

The key to constructing sentences that do the job is to know what job the words in a sentence do. That's a roundabout way of saying it helps to know the grammar. The verbose version of the manager's message contains twenty nouns, seven verbs and three pronouns. The concise version contains seven nouns, seven verbs and five pronouns.

Use fewer nouns

The verbose version doesn't work because it is overloaded with nouns. What is more, the nouns are nearly all abstract: 'position', 'regard', 'basis' and so on. The relatively few verbs, the words that should do most of the work, are weak, 'is', 'have' etc., and nearly all passive. The greater number of pronouns in the concise version is because it comes from people, 'We', and talks about people, 'we' and 'they', rather than using concepts like 'shortfall' and 'availability'.

Why do people write like this? Typically it happens when they represent organisations, rather than writing as individuals. Organisations are impersonal and focused on things like products, policies, structures and targets. Even when focused on people, they put them in categories like suppliers, voters, staff or customers. When you want to book a holiday, the airline will tell you whether they 'have availability'. When you complain about service, they'll say 'customer satisfaction is our highest priority'. Their focus is on things that can be measured. So when they write, they think first of nouns, often abstract ones, such as 'availability', 'satisfaction' and 'priorities', and then think of ways of linking them together. It's a kind of knitting with nouns. It tends to get tangled and, yes, woolly (Table 7.4).

Table 7.4 What do you see?

Abstract	Concrete
Downsizing	People losing their jobs
Collateral damage	Civilians being killed
Website content	Words and pictures
Sourcing content	Finding words and pictures
Embedment of new structures	Staff working well in new jobs

Be specific

Good, clear writing is like telling stories. It's about action and people, and mostly about specific things that you can visualise. Your aim is to transmit as clear a picture as you can to the other person. If someone tells you a boxer 'suffered brain damage', you get a picture of a person in a boxing ring or in hospital. That's already quite a strong picture, but if someone tells you instead that the boxer's 'brain was damaged', your mind's eye goes to his head, like a camera zooming in to the detail. A small change of words makes a dramatic difference.

The last bit of advice in this chapter is: concentrate on the verbs, using the active rather than passive voice, and choose concrete nouns as often as possible. If you need a reminder about what verbs, nouns and adjectives are, the next chapter should help.

Summary

Avoid jargon and slang and any words and phrases that exclude people.

Avoid cliches because they are second-hand phrases.

Choose short words, usually of German origin, over long words of Latin origin.

Express your ideas positively.

Talk about people and concrete things.

Concentrate on the verbs and make them active, not passive.

The functions of words

Parts of speech

Rules of grammar

Here we go into the jobs that words do. This brief review of grammar explains the main parts of speech – nouns, pronouns, verbs, adjectives and adverbs – as well as articles, prepositions and conjunctions.

Parts of speech

We are now looking at the jobs that words do; their grammatical function as opposed to their meaning. The word 'fast', for example, has different functions in 'I fast once a year' and 'He ends his fast when the sun sets'. In the first sentence it is a verb, expressing action, and in the second it is a noun, a thing. The meaning is the same, the function has changed.

Some jokes work by playing with the function of words. A legendary newspaper headline in the First World War read 'French push bottles up German rear'. The writer intended 'push' to be a noun meaning advance, but if 'push' is a verb it reads very differently.

In Chapter 7, we took a piece of bad writing, worked out what it was trying to say and then tried to express the same ideas more clearly. We ended up with far fewer nouns in proportion to verbs. One way of improving a piece of poor writing is to look at the nouns and see if you can convey the same meaning using a verb instead.

For example, you might be asked in a letter to 'supply the date of inheritance with regard to your holding of x'. As soon as you see 'with regard to', you know you're in for some turgid prose. The writer was forced to use it because he chose to use a noun 'inheritance' rather than the verb 'to inherit'. Having chosen a noun, the only way he could link the idea of inheriting to what was inherited was with the phrase 'with regard to'. Had he chosen the verb instead, he could have written 'the date you inherited your holding of x'. With the verb you go straight from the idea of inheriting to what was inherited. You don't need a woolly phrase to link them. You use fewer words to say the same thing and your meaning is clearer.

A simple analogy for the main parts of speech is a human body. The nouns are the bones. As the skeleton defines the shape and identity of the body, so the nouns are the things we write about, the subject matter, the hard bits. The verbs are the muscles, the bits that act, the dynamic part. The adjectives and adverbs are the fat. They are, as their names suggest, the add-on words. Adjectives add meaning to nouns and adverbs add meaning to verbs. A little fat is pleasing to the eye and the touch. Fat adds flavour to food and makes us feel good, but a lot of fat makes us flabby and unhealthy. The analogy is not perfect, but you can see where it leads: effective writing is muscular and dynamic, with just enough fat to give it a bit of flavour.

So:

1. Concentrate on the verbs. They are the key element in a sentence. They express action or a state of being.

2. Choose nouns that enable you to talk about real people and things wherever possible.

3. Be sparing with adjectives and adverbs. If you've chosen your nouns and verbs well, you shouldn't need many add-ons.

If you think of writing as a craft and words as your tools, you need to know them as well as you can. You need to be able to play with them, to try them in different combinations and orders. This means understanding what words mean and how they function grammatically. We all have an idea of how our language works. We absorb it and practise it from our earliest childhood. But if you are sure what function each word performs in a sentence, your writing will be much better than if you have only a rough idea. You can see from Table 8.1 how we are able to express the same ideas in different ways using different parts of speech. We don't always have a complete set of words, because language develops randomly according to how it is used, rather than systematically as if it were designed. Note, for example, that for an adverb expressing the idea of speaking we use 'orally' not 'spokenly'.

Test yourself. In the following sentence, identify one verb, four nouns and two adjectives.

The design provides a fisheye view of three levels of content.

The verb, expressing the action or state of being we are talking about, is 'provides'. The four nouns – in this case things as there are no people – are 'design', 'view' 'levels' and 'content'. The two adjectives are 'fisheye' and 'three'. Each adds meaning to one of the nouns in the sentence. What kind of 'view' do you get? It's a wider view than you get with a human eye without moving it. 'Fisheye' in this case is a noun being used as an adjective. How many levels can you see? 'Three'.

In this next sentence, there are two verbs, three nouns, two adjectives and one adverb.

A good website loads quickly and gives the user relevant information.

The verbs are 'loads' and 'gives'. The three nouns are 'website', user' and 'information'. The adjectives are 'good' and 'relevant'. The adverb, which adds meaning to the verb 'loads', is 'quickly'. In another sentence, 'loads' might have a different function. For example, in 'This website contains loads of information' 'loads' is a noun and the verb is 'contains'.

Table 8.1 How to say the same thing in different ways.

Noun	Verb	Adjective	Adverb
success	succeed	successful	successfully
use	use (pronounced uze)	useful/usable/used	usefully
rebel/rebellion	rebel (pronounced rebell)	rebellious	rebelliously
speech	speak	spoken	(orally)

One part of speech we have mentioned but not defined is the pronoun. As its name suggests, a pronoun stands in place of a noun. Using a pronoun instead of a noun makes sentences flow by avoiding irritating repetition. So instead of saying 'Joe found that Joe's website was bringing Joe a lot of business', we say 'Joe found that his website was bringing him a lot of business'. After we have established who we are talking about, replacing 'Joe' with a pronoun makes the sentence flow.

We'll go through the main parts of speech one by one, with some definitions, to help you make your writing as sharp as possible.

Nouns

Nouns (*n.* in the dictionary) are the names of people or things. They answer the questions Who? or What? They are either concrete or abstract. A person is concrete, in the sense of being real; and concrete things are animal, vegetable or mineral. Abstract nouns are ideas, concepts, things you can't touch. By abstracting your thoughts from real people and things, you are able to develop theories that you can then apply to all relevant situations, rather than starting from scratch every time. Abstract nouns are for talking about principles and theories. They should be kept in their place.

In much of life, abstract nouns tend to get in the way of understanding. They may even be used deliberately to distort the truth or to hide the fact that the writer has nothing to say. Usually they just create a fog. Why say 'Our preference would be for greater consistency in the appearance of the logo', using three abstract nouns? It would be clearer if you said 'We want the same logo on every page'. When stating the aim of your site, you may be tempted to get a bit philosophical and talk about 'enhancement' of this or that. It is probably better to choose concrete terms for what you are offering. Writing on websites for the most part should deal in real things that people can visualise and quantify.

Nouns are singular or plural. You are either talking about one person or thing, or several. It's obvious, but it's amazing how many sentences start by talking about one thing and end up talking about several, and vice versa, thus confusing the reader. Collective nouns are groups of things or people, such as the staff of a company. They usually count as a single noun. Again it's easy to find examples of writing where collective nouns start singular as in 'The staff is recruited from the surrounding area' and end up plural as in 'The staff frequently contribute to the website'. It's not a dreadful mistake; the meaning will be understood. But consciously or unconsciously the reader will be aware of an inconsistency. It shows the writer has not thought carefully enough about the ideas he or she wants to convey.

Proper nouns are particular people or things. We distinguish them by starting them with a capital letter. More about that in punctuation in Chapter 10.

Pronouns

As pronouns stand in for nouns, like nouns they also answer the questions Who? or What? Pronouns (*pron*. in the dictionary) are useful devices for referring to someone or something the second time you mention them. They help the flow of the writing by providing a kind of shorthand reference back. Instead of repeating a title and a name, for example the Chief Executive, Mary Bloggs, you just say 'she' the second time you mention her and the reader will know who you mean. The problems arise when you have been talking about her so long that the reader can't remember who she is. Two or three times is probably as much as a reader can cope with. And if you are talking about more than one person or thing, you need to be careful to avoid confusion.

The pronouns mentioned so far in this chapter are personal pronouns They are for referring to other people or things, for speaking in the third person (he, she, it, they): that is the language of description. On a website, we mostly want to use the language of dialogue, of conversation between two people. By starting off sentences with first and second person pronouns, notably 'we' and 'you', we establish a sense of dialogue between the website producer and the user.

Apart from personal pronouns, there are possessive pronouns (mine, yours, his, hers etc.) to use instead of repeating phrases such as 'the book belonging to me' and relative pronouns (who, which, whose) to link two statements instead of writing them as separate sentences. Other kinds of pronouns are indefinite (somebody, everybody), demonstrative (this, that) and interrogative (who? what? when? where? how?).

Adjectives

Adjectives (*a*. in the dictionary) describe people or things. They answer the question What is it (or he or she) like? They add meaning to nouns and pronouns.

The Simple Guide's advice is: be sparing with adjectives. Using a lot of them can be counterproductive. Instead of adding meaning to your nouns, they may dilute their meaning or confuse the reader. Take the example of 'a usual habit'. That's tautology because a habit is by definition usual. Adding 'usual' does not give extra weight to the idea you are trying to convey. On the contrary, it detracts attention from the noun and raises the possibility in the reader's mind that this habit may not be usual.

Using a lot of adjectives tends to draw attention to the descriptions rather than the things or people you are talking about. It's a kind of word-inflation and, as with real inflation, its effect is to devalue the currency. Calling things 'amazing', 'spectacular' or 'fantastic' is fine in conversation with friends, because we don't mean those words to be taken literally. All they tell our friends is that we like something. They are expressions of feeling, not fact. When you write, and especially when you write for people you don't know, your feelings are rarely relevant. You want to make your meaning clear and you need to use a stable currency.

Verbs
Verbs (*v.* in the dictionary) express doing or being. Without a verb, there is little or no meaning in a statement. In fact, if it hasn't got a verb in it we wouldn't call it a statement at all. Take political slogans. Three years after winning a huge majority in the general election of 1997, the Labour government was suddenly unpopular. The Prime Minister could no longer assume he had a huge lead in the opinion polls. The words that had seemed so powerful a short time before no longer carried any weight. One political commentator remarked

that Tony Blair was having to use verbs again: he was having to put meaning into his words. Slogans such as 'education, education, education' don't tell you much. They don't answer the question 'What are you doing about it?'

Verbs answer the question What? in the sense of 'What happened?', 'What did she do?' or 'What about it?'. If you walk into a room and exclaim 'My God, the cat!', the inevitable response will be 'What about the cat?' You have to say what you've done to it or what it has done, otherwise your exclamation does not mean much. The verbs are the key words in a sentence.

Whenever possible, use the active rather than the passive voice of the verb. In the sentence 'Our company makes widgets', the verb 'makes' is in the active voice. There is an action and you know who is doing it. In the passive voice it would be 'Widgets are made' and you do not know who by. The passive voice tells the story from the point of view of the person or thing to whom the action is done (Table 8.2).

Table 8.2 The active voice tells you more.

Passive	Active
Mistakes were found in the design	Warren found mistakes in the design
Steps have been taken to put it right	I have taken steps to put it right
The designer has been sacked	Elaine has sacked the designer
Warren and I will be given a bonus	Elaine will give Warren and me a bonus

Suppose you are involved in an incident in the street. If you say 'I was hit', you are using the passive. You have told us something and we have an idea of what happened to you, but you have missed out a vital piece of information: who or what did it. If you add that information in the passive voice it will be 'I was hit by the blue car'. Using the active voice, you can say the same thing using fewer words, 'The blue car hit me'. Because of the way verbs are constructed in English, the active voice tends to use fewer words to say the same thing. Just as important when you can use only a certain number of words in a particular space on a Web page, the active voice says more in the same number of words than the passive. Suppose it was a person, not a car, that hit you. In three words, the passive 'I was hit ' says only what happened to you. The active 'He hit me' says who did it as well.

If you wanted to tell a story from a particular person's point of view, you might be right to use the passive, but in many cases the passive is a sign of lazy writing. It suggests that the writer wants to do only half the work needed. Worse, it can be used deliberately to avoid commitment or evade responsibility. 'Every effort will be made to solve your problem' is not as reassuring as 'I will make every effort to ...' and 'An error was made in calculating your bill' leaves you fuming. Why can't they be honest and say 'We made an error'.

When you choose your verbs, remember the earlier advice to use a single word rather than a phrase whenever possible. Why say something 'was coincidental' when you have a perfectly good word, 'coincided'. Why 'stage an inquiry into' when you can simply 'investigate', and so on. The phrase is weaker than the single word.

Verbs have tenses – past, present, future, and some variations of these – to describe when an action takes place. Your tenses should be consistent so that the reader has a clear sense of the time of the actions you describe. 'He went to the site I had been working on' means he went there some time in the past and the 'I had' suggests that you are no longer working on the site. By contrast, 'He went to the site I have been working on' suggests you still are.

Agreement of tenses is especially important when reporting people's words. If you use the tenses correctly the reader knows exactly what was said. 'He said he would redesign the site' means that what he said was 'I will redesign the site'. If someone says 'I may do it' those words are in the present tense. If you report her words to someone else, her statement is in the past – she said it – so her words are moved one tense into the past: 'She said she might do it.'

Subject, verb and object
The verb has a subject, the doer or the person you are talking about. 'Subject' is a grammatical term which is not quite the same as what the sentence is about. It is quite precise: one word or phrase in a sentence is the subject of the verb. That word or phrase is a noun or pronoun, the person or thing performing the action. (Sometimes a part of a verb, like the participle 'having', is the subject of another verb and becomes in effect a noun, as in 'Having a website creates a lot of work'.) Take the verb 'to design'. If you say 'I design', 'design' is the verb and 'I' is the subject. Verbs often have objects, the thing or person the action is done to, to put it crudely. So in 'I design websites', 'I' is the subject, 'design' is the verb and the object is 'websites'.

This is the heart of the business of writing. If you can identify the building blocks – subject, verb, object – you can build anything you want. We 'construct' sentences (and 'build' websites). Writing is a craft that you can learn and practise. Choosing the right words is like choosing the right materials for your building. Constructing sentences is like putting the materials together so that the building will stand and looks good. To use another metaphor, understanding language is like understanding a piece of machinery by looking at it carefully, or even taking it to pieces, to see how it works. You wouldn't say that knowing how to mend a puncture took the fun out of bicycling; on the contrary, it should give you confidence.

Before we move on, there are a few more things to say about verbs. In the example above, 'I design websites', the verb 'to design' is used transitively, that is to say it has an object. When you say 'I design', you are using it intransitively, without an object: it makes sense on its own, answering the question 'What do you do?' You can do that with some verbs, but not all. You'll see them in the dictionary defined as transitive (*v.t.*) or intransitive (*v.i.*) or both (*v.t.* and *i.*). The verb 'to accuse' is transitive: it must have an object, you must accuse someone. The verb 'to rebel' is intransitive: you don't rebel anything, you just rebel. You may rebel against something, but that's different. That something is an indirect, not a direct, object so it does not make the verb transitive. An indirect object needs a word to link it to the subject, in this case 'against'.

Subject and verb must agree. This is easy in English compared with languages such as French or Russian. There's really only one question to ask: Is the subject singular or plural? Most verbs in English don't change much when you change the subject, grammatically speaking. They go 'I design', 'you design' and so on. The only one that is different is the third person singular, 'he designs'. If the subject is singular, 'the Web' for example, you must use the singular verb, 'is', whereas if the subject is plural, 'the Web pages' for example, the verb must be 'are'.

One reason we get it wrong is that, unlike the French or the Russians, we don't have to think much about subject-verb agreement, so we often don't think at all. Another reason is that if we make our sentences long and complicated, by the time we get to the verb we have forgotten what the subject was. For example, 'The project leader, whose views were decisive in the design of the pages, now that they are up and customers are buying more widgets, have decided to move on.' Putting a lot of information between the subject and verb is what causes the confusion, especially if, as in this case, the subject is singular and the noun just before the verb is plural.

Table 8.3 Subject and verb must agree.

Wrong	Right
A selection of laptops are available.	A selection of laptops is available.
It is you who is to blame.	It is you who are to blame.
Neither the colour nor the font are suitable.	Neither the colour nor the font is suitable.
What matters are results.	What matters is results. *or* Results are what matter.

Adverbs

After verbs come adverbs (*adv.* in the dictionary). They answer the question How? They are the easiest words to recognise in a sentence because most of them end in '-ly'. They describe actions. In grammatical terms, they qualify or modify verbs. They add meaning to verbs in the same way as adjectives add meaning to nouns. As with adjectives, the Simple Guide's advice is: be sparing. Don't devalue the currency.

If you find yourself using a lot of adverbs, you are probably choosing weak verbs and putting your meaning into the add-on words. The sentence 'This website works badly' uses a verb 'works' and an adverb 'badly'. The meaning is in the adverb, not the verb. A better sentence would be 'This website disappoints' or 'This website fails'. Here the meaning is in the verb and the sentence is shorter and clearer.

Those five – nouns, pronouns, adjectives, verbs and adverbs – are the main parts of speech. There are three minor ones to explain. Then we will have accounted for all the words in a sentence before we go on to constructing sentences.

Articles

Articles introduce nouns. In the dictionary, 'the', 'a' and 'an' are adjectives, but these adjectives are called articles. 'The' is the definite article, to be used when you want to refer to a particular thing or person. 'A' or 'an' is the indefinite article which you use when you are not referring to a particular one.

Prepositions

Prepositions (*prep.* in the dictionary) relate nouns and pronouns to other parts of speech. They are words that describe the relationship between other words.

In 'I was writing about your website', 'I was writing in your website' and 'I was writing for your website', the words 'about', 'in' and 'for' are prepositions describing different ways in which my writing relates to your website.

Conjunctions

Lastly, conjunctions (*conj*. in the dictionary) are words that link other words or groups of words. 'And', 'or' and 'but' are co-ordinating conjunctions, so called because they link words or groups of words that are equal in importance, grammatically speaking, as in 'safe and sound', 'fish or meat' and 'tough but tender-hearted'. Other conjunctions are called subordinating conjunctions because they link one group of words to another making one more important than the other. In 'make hay while the sun shines', the conjunction is 'while', 'make hay' is the main clause and 'while the sun shines' is the subordinate or dependent clause.

Rules of grammar

That's a brief look at the functions of words, the jobs they do. The rules are there to help make your writing effective. If you are sure something you are writing would be more effective if you broke a rule, then break it. There is a world of difference between breaking a rule of grammar for a good reason and using language ineffectively because you don't understand how it works. It is more important to keep in mind what you are trying to achieve than to remember all the rules. You can always look them up.

Summary

As well as knowing what words mean, you need to know their grammatical functions.

The main parts of speech are verbs, nouns, pronouns, adjectives and adverbs.

The verb is the key element in a sentence, expressing action or a state of being.

Nouns are people or things. Choose concrete rather than abstract nouns.

Pronouns replace nouns to avoid repetition.

Adjectives and adverbs are add-ons, to be used sparingly.

Nouns and pronouns are the subjects of verbs. Subject and verb must agree.

The active voice of the verb is shorter and more informative than the passive.

Articles, definite and indefinite, introduce nouns.

Prepositions relate nouns and pronouns to other parts of speech.

Conjunctions link words or groups of words.

Rules of grammar are there to help make your writing effective.

If you break them, do it for a good reason.

Constructing sentences

The right order

Sentences, phrases and clauses

Writing good sentences

Having taken the language to pieces, we now look at how to build the parts of speech into phrases, clauses and sentences. This chapter explains the importance of putting words in the right order and gives you advice on how to improve your sentences.

Choose the right words and put them in the right order. That's the advice for writing well. I've given you some rules for choosing words – words that accurately convey your meaning, single words rather than phrases, no jargon, no cliches, simple familiar words rather than long pompous ones, etc. We've broken the language down into its individual parts and defined their functions. Now we're dealing with how to put them together.

The right order

The order of words is more important in English than in many other languages. We had a hint of the difference between English and most other European languages when we were dealing with subject-verb agreement. In general, English words do not change their endings as they change their relationships with other words. You do not have to learn long lists of verbs and their endings, or nouns and theirs. For the most part, the only verb ending that differs from the others is the third person singular which has an 's' on the end. We say 'she writes', but 'write' for all the others – I, we, you, they. In French, each of those endings would be different. English nouns don't change endings at all. We don't change the ending of the word 'Moscow' according to whether we are going there or are there already. In Russian, we would have to.

The changing endings, or inflections, which existed in Old English mostly disappeared about 1000 years ago, as did the classification of nouns into masculine, feminine and neuter. The change made English grammar simpler and English a more flexible language. But it also made the order of words important. In Latin, you can write the words of a sentence in almost any order and the meaning is still clear because each word contains in itself its relationship to the other words. You have to use the correct form of each word to express your meaning. In English, however, 'Joe shot Peter' means one thing and 'Peter shot Joe' means something quite different. The meaning is dictated not by the words themselves but by the order you put them in.

While we're on the subject of inflections, as with all rules there are exceptions. English does retain a few words that change and they do cause problems. If we had used a pronoun in the example in the previous paragraph, we could not have changed the meaning just by changing the order. 'He shot Peter' could not be turned round to 'Peter shot he' because pronouns are some of the very few words left that do change according to their relationship to other words in the sentence. We would have to change 'he' to 'him'. 'I' is 'I' when it is the subject and 'me' when it is the object. 'You' stays the same. 'He' changes to 'him', 'she' changes to 'her', 'we' to 'us' and 'they' to 'them'.

The relative pronoun 'who', which becomes 'whom' when it is the object, is one that causes problems. In Chapter 2, I say the second of the three questions you should ask yourself before you start writing is 'For whom?' That is correct, though it does sound a bit pompous. Perhaps that's why some people think they are showing off their erudition by using 'whom'. Unfortunately they often get it wrong.

It is correct to say 'I saw the man whom I commissioned to set up the database'. The noun 'man' is the object of the verb 'saw' and the pronoun that you use for him in the subordinate clause is the object of the verb 'commissioned'. (Most of us would leave the relative pronoun out anyway and just say '… the man I commissioned …') It is not correct to say 'I saw the man whom I thought was setting up the database' because in this sentence the emphasis has shifted slightly. Whereas 'commissioned' is a transitive verb, 'thought' is intransitive:

it is almost in parenthesis. You wouldn't say 'I thought him was setting up the database', you would use 'he'. The man is now the subject of the verb in the subordinate clause, 'was setting up', so the relative pronoun should be 'who'.

We got into inflections, or the lack of them, in order to point out the importance of getting words in the right order. The rule is: put words next to, or as close as possible to, the words to which they relate most closely. Otherwise your meaning may be ambiguous.

The ambiguity may be serious, as in 'The judge ruled that statements made about the attack in court should not be broadcast', which leaves you not knowing whether it was the attack or the statement that was made in court. It may be comic, as in 'I know a man with a wooden leg called Mick', to which the reply comes 'Really. What's his other leg called?' Sometimes the mis-ordering just makes a sentence hard to follow, as in these instructions for setting up a computer: 'Make sure correct voltage shows in voltage switch window for your location.' It would be better as 'Make sure voltage switch window shows correct voltage for your location.'

In Figure 9.1, the phrase 'from this site' is in the wrong place, but moving it to where it belongs makes you wonder whether it is necessary anyway (Figures 9.2 and 9.3).

Sentences, phrases and clauses

If you get into a tangle trying to get the right words next to each other, you are probably trying to pack too much information into one sentence. Break up the information into two or more sentences. My advice, as in most writing manuals, is: keep your sentences short. It's not that you can't write good long sentences.

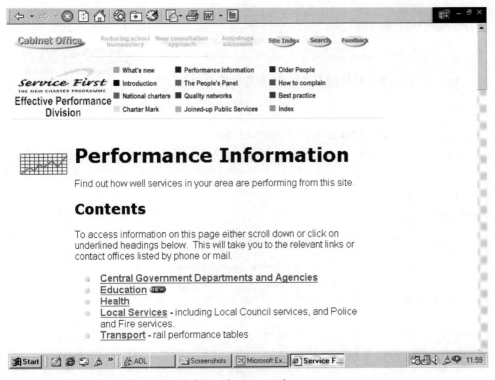

Figure 9.1 The phrase 'from this site' is in the wrong place.

It's just that the longer your sentences are, the greater the chance that something will go wrong.

Figure 9.2 Now 'from this site' is in the right place.

A sentence expresses a complete idea. A phrase does not. A clause may. A phrase is a group of words that functions as a single word. 'The background colour of my site' is a phrase. The words are in a certain order, so the phrase has meaning, but if you walked into a room and said it, it wouldn't make sense on its own. People would be waiting for more information. If you said 'The background colour on my site is yellow', the phrase would function as a noun and be the subject of the verb 'is' and you would have made a sentence.

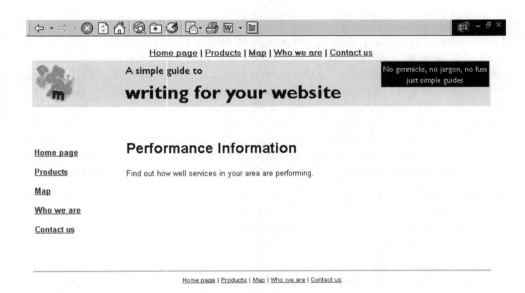

Figure 9.3 Was the phrase 'from this site' necessary at all?

A phrase may contain a verb or part of a verb, but not a finite verb, that is a verb with a subject. In 'having set up the home page', 'having set up' is a verb, or rather part of a verb, but the phrase does not make sense on its own. 'Having' is a participle: it cannot be a finite verb. You are waiting for the sentence to be completed, as in 'Having set up the home page, Sarah started thinking about the contacts page'. 'Having set up the home page' is a phrase which functions as a single word describing the activities of Sarah who is the subject of the verb 'started'.

A common fault in writing is using what's called a hanging participle or hanging clause or phrase. A famous example is 'After the Queen had named the ship, she slid gracefully into the water'. It's when you write a descriptive phrase and don't follow it with the person it applies to, as in 'Having set up the home page, the client told Sarah she didn't like it'. Grammatically, that means the client set up the home page. The meaning may become clear from the context, but there is an ambiguity there and you are expecting the reader to work out what you mean. You, the writer, should find another way of saying it, such as 'The client said she didn't like the home page Sarah had set up' or 'After all the work Sarah had put in to the home page, the client said she didn't like it'.

Starting every sentence with the subject can get monotonous. You will want to vary the rhythm of your writing by starting some sentences with a descriptive clause or phrase. Just make sure you place it next to the subject so that your meaning is unambiguous.

Unlike a phrase, a clause does contain a finite verb. It may make sense on its own or not. It depends how you use it. 'Although he improved the navigation on the site' is a clause. It contains a finite verb, 'improved', whose subject is 'he', but it does not make sense on its own. The first word 'although' tells you that you are waiting for more information. So it is called a subordinate or dependent clause: it depends on another clause to complete the idea. 'Although he improved the navigation on the site, he continued to get complaints' is a sentence. The clause we added, 'he continued to get complaints', is the main clause of the sentence. A main clause makes sense on its own.

A sentence consisting of one clause, a main clause, is called a simple sentence. A sentence with two or more equal clauses is called a compound sentence. A sentence with a main clause and one or more subordinate clauses is called a complex sentence. Those are grammatical terms, but they fit well with the thrust of advice in the Simple Guide: keep your writing simple. Compound and complex sentences require the reader to keep several bits of information in mind at once. The longer and more complicated a sentence is, the greater the chance that the reader will lose the thread or misunderstand the information. On your home page and the pages immediately below, where your text is sparse and the user is scanning for information, simple sentences are almost a must. Further in, where your text is denser and the user is into something they have chosen to read, you can and should vary the rhythm of your writing with a mixture of simple, compound and complex sentences. Compare Figures 9.4 and 9.5.

Writing good sentences

There are one or two other tips for writing good sentences. The first is: keep the same subject throughout a sentence. That makes it easier to follow. A simple sentence has only one clause and therefore only one subject. The problem comes when you put several ideas into one sentence. Changing subject in the middle of a sentence forces the reader to make an extra mental effort to follow your train of thought (Table 9.1).

Another way of making your sentences flow is to express the ideas in them in a similar way. That often means using the same parts of speech – verbs, nouns or adjectives. The sentence 'I opposed the project because of the cost and the manager disliked me' uses a noun to express one objection, the cost, and a verb to express the other, the manager disliked me. It doesn't flow well. It would be better to say either '… because it was going to cost millions and the manager disliked me' or '… because of the cost and the fact that the manager disliked me'. Then the ideas are balanced and easier to follow.

Figure 9.4 A string of simple sentences on one topic makes hard reading.

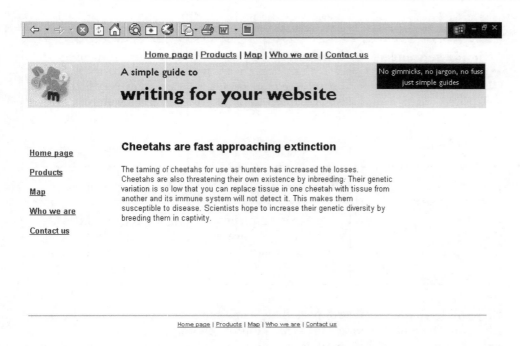

Figure 9.5 Once you're into details you can vary the rhythm of your writing.

The third thing to think about in your sentences is where to place the important words. Just as supermarkets have developed a science of placing goods where they are most likely to be bought, so writers should place words where

Table 9.1 Changing subject in the middle of a sentence makes it hard to follow.

Simple sentence	Compound sentence	Complex sentence
I want to commission a website.	I want to commission a website and I want you to design it.	As I know very little about designing websites, I'd like you to design my new site.
	Changing subject	**Changing subject**
	I want to commission a website and you are the person to design it.	As I know very little about designing websites, you would be the best person to design my new site.

they will have the greatest impact. The prime spots in a sentence are the beginning and the end. If you get into the habit of reading your work out loud, you will be aware of the rhythm of your sentences and the importance of ending on a strong word or phrase, rather than tailing off on a weak one. On a website, where your text is likely to be shorter and more broken up than in print, the first and last words of your sentences or paragraphs are more exposed.

Summary

Put your words in the right order: next to, or as close as possible to the words they relate to.

If you find it hard to put the right words next to each other, put them in separate sentences.

A sentence expresses a complete idea. It must contain a finite verb.

A sentence with one clause is a simple sentence; with more than one it is a compound or complex sentence.

Keep your sentences short.

Don't use a lot of subordinate clauses.

Keep the same subject throughout a sentence.

Try to make sentences flow by expressing ideas in a similar way.

Place important words at the beginning and the end.

Spelling and punctuation

Spelling old and new

The Simple Guide's style

Punctuation

We take a quick look at spelling and a rather longer one at punctuation. This chapter contains definitions of the punctuation marks you will need and advice on how to use them. Spelling and punctuation are big issues on a website because of the importance of the way the text looks.

Spelling old and new

'Commynycacyon.' That's how William Caxton spelled 'communication' more than five hundred years ago. When he set up the first printing press in England, Caxton had to decide which of many versions of English spelling to use. Some of his decisions are with us today, though 'commynycacyon' is not one of them. It took several hundred years for English spelling to be standardised. Even in the 20th century it was still changing. The preface to the 1911 Concise Oxford Dictionary had 'inflexion' and Shakspere' rather than the current 'inflection' and 'Shakespeare'.

The idea, however, of having to work out what individual writers mean by their own ways of spelling is long gone. We expect everyone to write words in the same way and we expect to be able to recognise words immediately. All the more so with the speed of communication now. Just as the layout, navigation, links and other features of websites have quickly become standardised, so the language used on a site should be standardised in order to be instantly recognisable.

A website is undermined by mistakes or inconsistencies in spelling. Users don't necessarily notice every mistake, but consciously or unconsciously they register an inconsistency which undermines their confidence in the site.

Beware the computer spellchecker. It may draw your attention to mistakes and encourage you to re-read your text, but you can't rely on it. Volumes could be written about the mess it gets you into, quite apart from the laziness it induces. It inspired this poem in a flight magazine:

I have a spelling checker. It came with my PC.
It plainly marks four my revue mistakes I cannot sea.
I've run this poem threw it. I'm sure your please to no
Its letter perfect in it's weigh. My checker tolled me sew.

Far better to keep your own editorial eye sharp and a dictionary beside you. Once you have decided what spelling to adopt, stick to it.

For the most part, you can rely on a dictionary, but on very recent additions to the language you may have to decide for yourself. You've probably noticed that there is as yet no agreed spelling of many of the words we use on websites. Should it be 'website' or 'Web site'? How do you spell 'online'? Some people write 'on-line'. Sometimes it is 'on line'. And the companies that work on the Web are described in a variety of ways – 'dot com', 'dot-com' , 'dotcom' or even 'dot.com'.

The Simple Guide's style

In this Simple Guide, I start 'Web' with a capital letter because it is a proper noun: there is only one Web. I write 'Web pages' to distinguish them from printed pages, but 'websites' because there are no other sites to confuse them with: websites have become a distinct class of thing. I write 'online', both for the adjective in 'online shopping' and for where you are when you use a website. Although it might be more logical to write 'I am on line', the meaning is not as obvious as it is in 'I am online'. When you say it, you will probably put the stress on the second syllable, 'line', whereas in the adjective you would put it on the first syllable, 'on'.

I favour 'dotcom'. It's a new expression combining an existing word 'dot' and an abbreviation of an existing word 'com'. The two parts need to be tied together to form an adjective and it doesn't seem to fit the usual argument for a hyphen. What about 'email'? It is more difficult as it is a combination of a single letter with a word. Quite a lot of people write 'e-mail'. Should we write 'e-commerce' or 'ecommerce'? I put 'email' all in one, but hyphenate 'e-commerce'. The reason is that, while 'email' may not be universal, it is not likely to be misread; whereas 'ecommerce' starts the same way as a lot of other words, such as 'economic' and 'ecology', and could be misread. That is the criterion. We are talking about how to spell and mark words so as to make them immediately recognisable.

Punctuation

It helps to think of punctuation as marks that you put on a piece of writing to remove any ambiguity. You have chosen the best words you can and put them in the right order. The punctuation is the finishing touch. Just to show what punctuation can do, take these words and see what they mean to you:

> woman without her man is an empty vessel

Without punctuation, it is one sentence with 'woman' as the subject, so it means a woman is incomplete without a man. With punctuation, you can reverse the meaning:

> Woman! Without her, man is an empty vessel.

Punctuation is a powerful tool. Many legal documents are deliberately written without commas because the difference that a comma can make to an inheritance or a dispute is so great that some lawyers think it is safer to do without them than to risk putting one in the wrong place. There is an argument for using as little punctuation as possible on websites, but it has to do with the visual impression rather than legal arguments. A lot of punctuation marks can make a Web page look messy.

Capital letters

The standard uses of capital letters are at the beginning of a sentence and at the beginning of names of particular people and things – proper nouns. So this sentence starts with a capital 'S' and the Simple Guide has capital 'S' and 'G' because it is the name of this particular book and references to it should stand out in the text. The point of capital letters is to draw the reader's eye to the start of something important. Capitals should be used sparingly, otherwise the eye gets confused.

Avoid writing text in capital letters; a title perhaps, and some headings, but no sentences or long bits of text. We tend to recognise the shapes of words and sentences rather than read every letter. We find it hard to read words written entirely in capitals because we are used to reading text that is mostly in lower case with a few capitals as highlights. The irony is that in text where writers put important information in capitals precisely to draw our attention to it, we tend to skip it (compare Figures 10.1 and 10.2).

You need to be particularly careful about using too many capitals on a website because the text is broken up and you tend to have more headings and titles than you do in printed text. The convention in print is that every word in a title starts with a capital letter. This is all right when a title is three words long. Once you have more than three words, a title begins to lose its impact if every word starts with a capital. One thing you can do is not to use a capital on the minor words such as 'and', 'or' and 'with'. In general it's a good idea to use as few capitals as possible, so that the ones you do use indicate the important words.

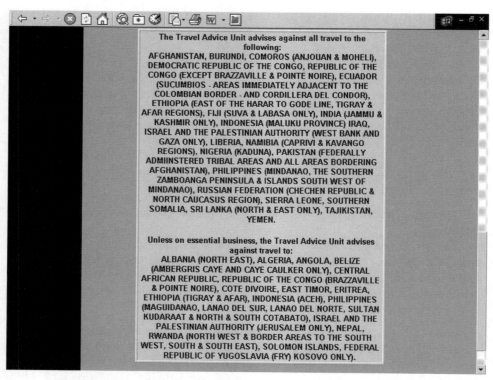

Figure 10.1 Blocks of text in capital letters are difficult to read.

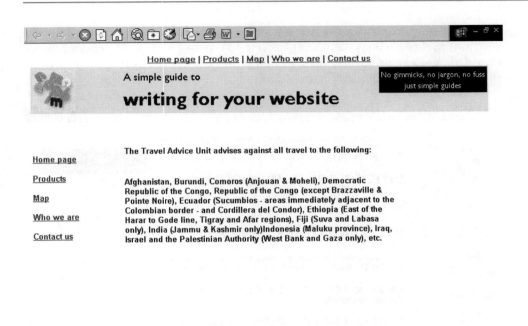

Figure 10.2 Text with capitals used sparingly is easier on the eye.

Bold and other devices

The same goes for other devices that draw attention – changes of font or colour, different sizes of font, italics, underlining and bold or highlighting (or strong in

HTML). Underlining is out because it might be confused with a link. As for the rest, use them sparingly. Their function is to create contrast. If you emphasise everything, you emphasise nothing, and if you use too many different devices, the user ends up confused (Figure 10.3).

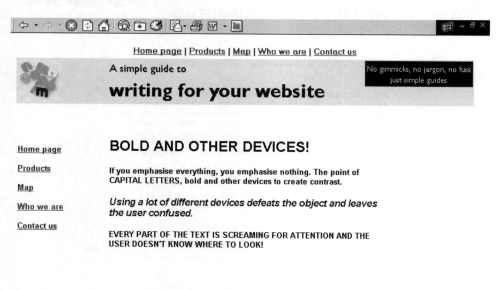

Figure 10.3 Devices that draw attention should be used sparingly.

Full stops and other endings

We mark the end of a sentence with a full stop, an exclamation mark or a question mark. Like capitals, exclamation marks and question marks are emphatic marks and should be used sparingly. Exclamation marks can suggest that writers are showing off or are not sure their words will be taken the right way. A lot of exclamations and questions on a screen can be tiresome.

Don't be afraid of full stops, however. With some text, you feel you can see the writers punctuating as they go along and simply putting a dash or comma every time they pause, as though they were frightened of losing the reader by putting a full stop. If what you have said makes sense on its own, if it expresses a complete idea, put a full stop and start another sentence. Forcing yourself to write in sentences is a good discipline. Trying to do without dashes, and even commas, makes you think carefully about what you are writing.

Points

The full stop is also known as a point. We use single points to show when words have been abbreviated, as in e.g. This is another device for making text understandable first time. If you write e.g. as 'eg', there's always a chance that the eye may not recognise it and read it as if it sounds like 'egg'. A lot of points have disappeared from abbreviations in the past few years. BBC is short for British Broadcasting Corporation, but the BBC no longer calls itself the B.B.C. Many companies, as they have grown and changed their core businesses, acquiring and shedding other companies along the way, first changed their names to abbreviations and then got rid of the points. That left them with names consisting of two or three letters that did not identify the company with a particular enterprise and had the advantage of being easier for designers to work with.

Ellipsis

Three points together are known as an ellipsis. They show that words have been left out. If you are quoting someone, using an ellipsis allows you to use the best parts at the length you want. It has the advantage of suggesting that you are taking the trouble to quote accurately.

The ellipsis has come to mean 'and so on'. Microsoft, for example, uses it in menus. The menus show a few items followed by '...' and users know that if they hold on, a longer list will come up. It has become common on websites to use this mark to tell the user that there is more to come. The ellipsis is meant to entice you by keeping a visual thread of communication going. However, while it does entice, it would be better if the words did the job on their own. It's as if the writer does not have confidence in the words he or she has chosen. At its worst, the ellipsis gives the impression that the writer can't be bothered to finish the sentence and is in effect saying 'you know the rest'.

Commas

The comma, as lawyers have found, can cause problems. There are no hard rules for when to use a comma, although you should not use one when you should be using a full stop. The Simple Guide's advice is: use commas sparingly. If your sentences are mostly short and crisp, you shouldn't need many commas. It's a good idea to choose your words first, then put in commas where they are needed to prevent ambiguity. The commas should help the sense of the words and not hinder the flow. Use commas to mark pauses, as we have in this sentence to separate two clauses.

Commas in lists replace 'and'. Rather than write 'design and colour and text', we write 'design, colour and text'. In a list of single words you should not need a comma before 'and'. In general, you don't need a comma before 'and', but in a longer, more complicated list you may want one to make it clear. Even in a simple list, you may use a comma to emphasise the last item, as in 'He was rude, untidy, and inefficient'. If your descriptive words are not a list, you don't need a comma. For example, in 'an untidy young man' the two adjectives progressively describe the man more precisely, with the more general 'young' being next to the noun. It would be wrong to separate them with a comma as though you might have used 'and' instead. You would not say 'He is an untidy and young man'.

Use commas in pairs to mark words that add information that is not essential to the sentence. You should put a pair of commas round a short description, as in 'John Smith, the famous actor, is appearing this week at the Magnifico Theatre'. The phrase 'the famous actor' adds information, but is not essential. In the sentence 'The comma, as lawyers have found, can cause problems', the commas are round the subordinate clause. Without the words between the commas, you have a simple sentence, 'The comma can cause problems'. On the other hand, don't make the mistake of putting commas round words that are necessary to the meaning of the sentence, as in 'Actors, who forget their lines, are always booed by the audience'. And don't confuse the reader by forgetting the second comma in a pair, as in 'The World Wide Web, which was invented by Tim Berners-Lee has grown at an astonishing rate'.

Parentheses
You can use brackets and pairs of dashes in the same way as pairs of commas. It's called putting words or information in parentheses. You can also use brackets to mark off a whole sentence as not essential.

Semi-colons

There is a hierarchy of pause marks. The comma is the lowest, the semi-colon next, then the colon and then the full stop. The semi-colon marks a slightly longer pause than a comma, but if you write short sentences you will not often need it. Its main use is when you have a list within a list, as in 'The Simple Guide covers the peculiarities of the Web; the purpose of your website; who it's for and what it's about; grammar, spelling and punctuation.' You may want to use a list like that in the body of some text, but if the list is an important one, high up the hierarchy of your site, you are more likely to use bullet points (which we go into in some detail in Chapter 13). The semi-colon has the drawback of being hard to read on a screen.

Colons

As with the semi-colon, you won't need the colon much if you are writing short sentences. The traditional use of the colon is to tie together two clauses that could stand alone as separate sentences, where the second is a development of the first. For example, 'The Simple Guide makes writing easy: it is full of examples.' The colon tells the reader that the second clause illustrates the idea expressed in the first. A much more common use for the colon is to introduce a list, as in 'The Simple Guide helps you with all aspects of writing for the Web: the peculiarities of the Web, the purpose of your website etc'. So you will often use a colon to introduce bullet points.

The Simple Guide uses a colon to introduce short bits of advice. Earlier in this chapter I said 'The Simple Guide's advice is: use commas sparingly.' This is to emphasise the advice by putting quite a strong pause before it. I could have used a stronger device, such as bold or italics or perhaps a dash.

Dashes

The dash is used at the end of a sentence to make an impact. Rather than write 'We know what the result will be. It will be a disaster', you make a more dramatic statement if you write 'We know what the result will be – disaster'. It's a useful device for summing up at the end of a sentence, though if you use it in that way it means you have written a pretty long sentence. Don't fall into the trap, as some writers do, of using the dash as an all-purpose punctuation mark. It is not a substitute for a full stop, nor usually for a comma or either of the marks in between. Keep it for a specific purpose and it will be effective. Using a lot of dashes on websites makes the pages look messy.

Hyphens

A hyphen has a quite different function from a dash, though the mark itself is the same in most fonts and on most keyboards. The dash creates a dramatic pause because it has space around it. The hyphen ties words together: it has no space around it. Too many dashes confuse the eye. Well placed hyphens help the eye read the text correctly.

There are lots of anecdotes to illustrate the importance of hyphens. There's 'extra-marital sex', which without a hyphen would mean more sex within marriage. There's the story about the company that forgot its hyphens when ordering rods: instead of 'six-foot-long rods', it received 'six foot-long rods'. As you can see from these examples, hyphens are mostly needed when two or more words are turned into an adjective and put before a noun. Those words may be a verb. When you 'set up' a business, you don't need a hyphen, but when you refer to the 'set-up costs', you do.

When you talk about private money for projects in the public sector, you may refer to 'projects financed by private money' or 'privately financed projects'. Neither phrase needs punctuation because the meaning is unambiguous. In the latter, 'privately' is an adverb modifying the verb 'financed', so needs no hyphen. If, however, you refer to 'private-sector finance' you have used the phrase 'private sector' as a single adjective, so there should be a hyphen to tie the two words together. Otherwise you might be talking about sector finance that is private, which is nonsense.

In speech, the meaning of 'private-sector finance' is made clear by the way the words are stressed, but what about a 'fine-tooth comb'? It is almost universally stressed as if there were a hyphen between 'tooth' and 'comb', as if there existed an instrument for combing teeth or as if there could be a comb that did not have teeth. If it's a comb with fine teeth, the hyphen should go between 'fine' and 'tooth'.

If you see the phrase 'hard working man' on its own, you aren't sure where to put the stress. It could be a man who works hard, in which case 'hard' and 'working' should be hyphenated, otherwise it must be a working man who is hard. The ambiguity in this example is because 'hard' can change functions. You don't usually need hyphens between an adverb and a verb, because there is usually no possibility of confusion. In this case, 'hard' applied to 'working' is an adverb, so would not usually need a hyphen, but because it could be mistaken for a second adjective applied to 'man', you need a hyphen to make your meaning clear.

Hyphens are particularly helpful in writing where definitions are of the essence, as in science or medicine. If you describe a mammal as a 'small fish eater', the reader needs to know whether it is small and eats fish or eats only small fish. Imagine a non-specialist trying to understand 'high-speed fibre-optic rings' without hyphens. In medical writing it is important to ascribe causes correctly as in 'cancer-related ailments' and to avoid ambiguity as in 'patient-friendly contraception'.

Apostrophes

The apostrophe has two functions. It indicates possession, as in 'John's computer', and it indicates where words have been contracted to leave letters out, as in 'don't' for 'do not'. If you are confused by the apostrophe, you are not alone. One reason for confusion is that although the apostrophe indicates possession in nouns, it is not used in possessive pronouns and adjectives, many of which end in 's'. So it is not used in 'yours', 'his', 'hers', 'its', 'ours' or 'theirs'. One tip for remembering that rule is to think of them as a group. You wouldn't think of putting an apostrophe in 'mine', or in 'his', so don't put one in 'its'.

The other place you should not put an apostrophe is in a plural. Again the confusion arises because we mostly use the letter 's' to make a noun plural. 'Books', 'potatoes' and 'websites' don't need apostrophes. Just occasionally you may need to use them to prevent words being misread. 'Mind your p's and q's' is a rare case where apostrophes in plurals are justified. Another is 'do's and don'ts' and it's a good example of putting the purpose above the rule. Without an apostrophe, the first word might be read as 'doss', but a second apostrophe in 'don'ts' would confuse rather than clarify. No consistency here: what matters is that people read the words right first time.

Quotation marks

The last punctuation marks we deal with are quotation marks or inverted commas. The Simple Guide uses lots of quotation marks, because I have illustrated my advice as much as possible. That raises questions about how to punctuate the examples. Where the quotation is a sentence or more, I have put it into a separate paragraph in a different font, but without quotation marks. Short quotations I have kept within a paragraph and put in quotation marks. The convention when quoting is to put a comma before you open the quotation marks, though that usually applies to statements rather than single words or short phrases. I decided against putting a comma before quotations within a paragraph because it would break the flow of the argument and make the text look messy.

I've used single quotation marks rather than double, again to avoid cluttering the text. On a website, single quotation marks tend to look tidier. It's not a good idea to use quotation marks to indicate sarcasm. Trying to replicate the tone of someone's voice doesn't usually work. If you find yourself waggling your fingers in the air to show that you are quoting, it probably means you are not comfortable with the words you are using and should think again.

The finishing touch

Punctuation is one of the devices at your disposal to help make up for the deficiencies of writing, as opposed to speaking, as a means of communication. But it should be a last resort. Try to make your choice of words and the order you put them in do as much work as possible. Use only those punctuation marks that are necessary to make your meaning clear. On a screen your text is briefer and more broken up than on a printed page and punctuation marks tend to make it look untidy.

Summary

Mistakes in grammar or spelling make your website less credible.

It's best to check your own text, rather than relying on a spellchecker.

Punctuation marks tend to make a website look messy, and should be left out if possible.

Attention-seeking devices – capitals, bold etc.– only work if you use them sparingly.

Full stops mark the ends of sentences. Dashes or commas won't do.

Ellipsis (...) means words have been left out. Most other uses are sloppy.

Commas mark pauses in sentences and separate items in lists.

Pairs of commas, dashes or brackets (parentheses) mark off inessential material in a sentence.

Semi-colons mark stronger pauses than commas. They don't show up well on a screen.

Colons are mostly used to introduce lists.

A single dash can create a dramatic pause at the end of a sentence.

Hyphens help the reader by tying the right words together.

Apostrophes indicate possession or show that letters have been left out.

Quotation marks are for quoting, and should not be used ironically.

How does it look?

Where to write

How to lay out the text

Headings

This chapter looks at how to make the best use of the words on your website. We look at layout in general, columns, justification, fonts, colours, paragraphs, headings and side-headings. We are straying into design, but as a writer you need to know about presentation.

For all the attention given to the design of websites – the images, colours and animations – it's the words that count. Research that has tracked the eye movements of Web users suggests that they tend to look for words rather than images and manage to ignore altogether some images that are designed to attract their attention. They even ignore bits of information that look like advertisements, but aren't. That research by the Stanford-Poynter project in the United States was done on news sites, so you would expect a bias towards words. You might also say that words are bound to attract more attention than images because when you go into a website the words usually appear on the screen first. Besides, the images on a website are less clearly defined than they would be in print, so they tend to have less impact. Even with all these qualifications, the finding that users went for the words rather than the images is instructive.

Where to write

When we first look at a screen, our eyes tend to focus somewhere in the middle, about a third of the way down. Because our language reads from left to right and top to bottom, we expect text to start somewhere on the left near the top. That is where your most important words should go. Some of your screen will be taken up with navigation. Unlike a book, newspaper or other printed publication, a website has to have navigation on every page to help the user understand the site, and the navigation usually goes down the left side or across the top, or both. The right side of the screen may not be visible to the user at first and you want the user to get your message without having to scroll across or down. That leaves an area roughly 12×15 centimetres, or 30 square inches, for you to write in.

It is not a good idea to make the text run right across the screen. The longer the line of text, the more the eye has to move and the more difficulty it has finding its way from the end of one line to the beginning of the next. The screen is wider than a page of most books. In wide books, the text is usually confined to the middle with space on either side or to one side with illustrations on the other. The pages of newspapers and magazines are wider still, but they are divided into columns.

Devices such as columns make it easy for the eye to take in information with as little movement as possible. When you read, you mostly recognise whole words rather than read every letter. If you read fast, you recognise whole phrases or even sentences. There is a happy medium between running the text right across the screen and forcing it into columns so narrow that you cannot see the shapes of the phrases or sentences, as happens in some newspapers and websites. That means starting your main text left of the middle of the screen and making it not more than half the width of the screen. 10–12 words, roughly 50–70 characters, make a line a comfortable length to read (Figure 11.1).

How to lay out the text

Your main text should be somewhere in the middle, but it's better not centred. Centred text makes for messy lists and lines that are hard to read when each one starts and ends in a different place (Figure 11.2). Research suggests that we read most easily when the text is left-justified, with every line starting at the same point on the left, but not fully justified (*Plain English Handbook*). It is tempting to write text that is both left- and right-justified because it looks tidy, as in traditional printing. But in traditional printing words are carefully hyphenated to fit the width of the column or page, whereas full justification in

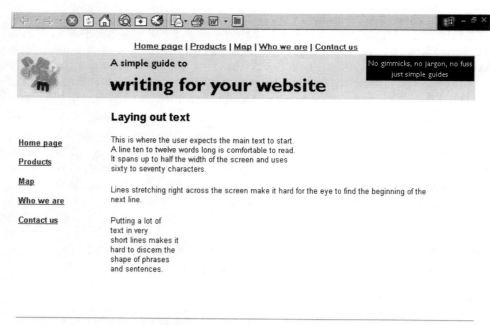

Figure 11.1 Laying out text on a website so that it is comfortable to read.

Figure 11.2 Centred text is difficult to read.

most word processors varies the spaces between letters and words to fit the width. This stretching and compressing of words confuses the eye. The Simple Guide's advice is: justify your text on the left (in other words left-align it) and leave it ragged on the right (Figure 11.3).

Figure 11.3 Left-aligned text is the easiest to read.

Fonts

My advice about fonts and colours is also based on research into how people read most easily. In general, the eye finds it easier to read fonts with serifs, such as Times, the serif being the little bit added to the top left and bottom right of most letters. The serifs have the effect of leading the eye from the end of one letter to the beginning of the next. In print, serif fonts are used for the majority of text. On a screen, other considerations come into play. The screen uses fewer dots per inch than print. Letters are much less clearly defined. So the serif fonts, rather than helping the eye, may burden it by looking fuzzy.

Many professionally designed websites use fonts without serifs, known as sans-serif fonts, such as Arial. The general rule has come to be: serif for print, sans-serif for screen. But it is not as simple as that. Many sans-serif fonts were developed for headlines or posters and were not intended for text. If your site has relatively little text and what there is is in small chunks, sans-serif will work well. But if you have a lot of text and especially if you expect the user to print what you have written rather than read it on screen, your text will be easier to read in a serif font. Sites with a lot of text often compromise, as do many printed texts. They use a sans-serif font for the headings and side-headings (and navigation) where the user is scanning the page for the key information, and a serif font for the body of the text where the user has focused their attention and wants to read (Figure 11.4).

Another consideration is space. Although serif fonts may not be as clear on the screen as sans-serif fonts, they are more compact. A sans-serif font can be made more readable by spacing it out, but then it will take up even more space and space is at a premium on Web pages. That's one reason why Times New Roman (which was specially developed for the computer screen) is the default font on most browsers.

Apart from functional considerations, there's the character of a font. Your choice of font says something about you and what you are offering on your website. Successful sites tend to be those with a distinct personality. You might not use the same font to sell computer accessories as you would to discuss antiques or compare different ways of planting a vegetable garden, for instance. In the end you will weigh up all these considerations, try different fonts on screen and decide for yourself.

Figure 11.4 Mixing serif and sans-serif fonts.

Colours

The clearest text is in black letters on a white background. That is too dull for many people, but the rule must be to make your font and background colours as distinct from one another as you can. Quite a few sites use white text on a black background. Some use white on a strong colour. It depends what counts as strong. White on green is reckoned all right; white on red is not. Unfortunately I can't show you here, but take a look at different sites to see what works. Once you are into colours, you have to consider things such as the fact that only a few colours look the same in every browser. We have strayed into the territory of the design manuals, but as a writer you have an interest in your words being as clear as possible on the screen and you need to have your own ideas as to what works and what doesn't.

After a brief look at fonts and colours, we come back to the layout of the main text. So far my advice has been: use left-justified, right-ragged text starting to the left of middle and taking up not more than half the width of the screen. Next are paragraphs and headings.

Paragraphs

We break up text to make it easier to take in. The way we break it up reflects the way we have organised the information we are offering. Many Victorian novels were divided into chapters equivalent to the amount of text that a man might read to his family in an evening or the amount that made a coherent chunk of narrative when the novel appeared in instalments in a magazine. That meant chapters of similar length consisting of dense text usually appearing under a single heading.

There is no standard unit for dividing text on a website. The information is broken up into many pieces of many different lengths, from three-word headings to many-thousand-word articles, depending on where you are in the hierarchy of the site. There are different considerations on the home page and pages at various other levels. Yet many of the principles of laying out text in a way that makes it easy to read are similar to those for print.

What makes a paragraph easy to identify is not the words in it but the space around it. In print that is called white space and for some the convention has carried over into websites, even though the space may be yellow or black. The amount of white space will depend on where you are in the hierarchy of the site: it will usually be more on the home page and the pages immediately below it, and less the further down you go.

You need space on either side of text, in the form of margins, and you will usually put space between paragraphs. For years, the convention was to indent paragraphs. That works well in dense continuous text: the indentation marks the beginning of a new paragraph. The introduction of word processing, however, has allowed documents to be created much more easily and to be laid out in many different ways. Anyone with a word processor can publish documents. There is more playing around with layout and more extravagant use of paper. With more white space on the page, indenting paragraphs does not work so well. It is now usual instead to put a line space between paragraphs and to align the first word of each paragraph to the left.

On a website, it is vital for the eye to be able to identify the main elements of the information quickly. Finding the start of paragraphs is one of the key ways of doing this. Putting margins on either side and space between paragraphs makes each paragraph stand out as a block. Rather than having to look along the first line for the indentation, it is easier for the eye to find the start of the paragraph at the top left corner of each block.

Headings

The same goes for headings. When text is dense and justified, as it is in many books and magazines, it makes sense to centre the title or headline to make it stand out above the text. Where text is broken up by a lot of white space, however, a centred heading can look lost. I have recommended that you justify your text on the left and leave it ragged on the right. If you align your heading with the text, you are creating a vertical line on which each new bit of information starts, thus making it easier for the user to read what you write. A heading should not take up more than one line and will usually be between three and seven words long.

Side-headings

Paragraphs are blocks of text that look easier to read than continuous prose. By taking the trouble to divide up your text, you show that you are trying to help the reader. But it's not an arbitrary division. There is an interplay between the visual requirements and the organisation of your thoughts. Having to divide your text into paragraphs makes you think about the way your information is structured. Each paragraph should have a single topic. A paragraph may consist of a single sentence. In print, paragraphs may run to ten sentences, but in a website they will usually be three or four sentences long. Paragraphs are easier to read if each sentence has the same grammatical subject too.

Side-headings are the subject of this paragraph. Side-headings help the user as they scan the page for information. They may consist of a single word or up to seven. For visual impact they should be less than half the width of the text they sit above. As well as helping the user scan the page, they help you clarify your thoughts. Side-headings help you answer the question 'What is this paragraph about?', as opposed to the paragraph before or the one after.

Summary

You have an area less than half the size of the screen to write in.

The prime position is left of centre, near the top.

Your text should be no more than half the width of the screen.

Centred text is hard to read, as is fully justified text.

Text that is left-justified and ragged on the right is easiest to read.

As a general rule serif fonts are easier to read, but sans-serif fonts look better on a screen.

Text and background colours should be as distinct from one another as possible.

Web text is broken up into pieces of different lengths according to where you are in the site.

Text on the home page will usually be sparse; further in the site it will be denser.

Paragraphs, headings and side-headings should be left-justified.

Dividing your text into paragraphs makes you structure your information.

Writing side-headings above paragraphs makes your text easy to scan.

Writing your home page

Describe yourself and your purpose

Engage the user

Describe what you are offering

Describe how to get it

Invite contributions

Put your best bits first

Here we look at the things every home page must do: identify you and your site, engage the user, make clear what you are offering and help the user find it. Some of the advice, for example about writing links, applies to other pages as well.

The words on the home page are what your site is about. They may be only two or three dozen, but they are the most important words in the whole site. Remember that the user cannot see your site in the way that a reader can see and hold and thumb through an entire book or magazine in a few moments. In the few seconds you have before the user becomes impatient or confused or bored, the words on your home page must do several things. They must identify you and your site, engage the user, make clear what you are offering, and help the user find it.

Describe yourself and your purpose

It is worth spending a good deal of time thinking about and finding the right words. The few words you come up with to describe yourself and your purpose will become the key words at the top of your home page and possibly all your other pages too. Remember to include the page title (<title> in HTML). The words you write in the title, which appears above your page in the bar at the top of the screen, are often the first words the user sees when your home page comes up. If your page takes time to load, they may be the only words the user sees for several seconds. Perhaps even more important, they are the words that are used by some search engines to identify your page and the words that will appear in a user's list of bookmarked or favourite pages.

Test some sites yourself at random. Which were the sites you really liked, as opposed to the ones you thought looked good? The answer is often the ones with a clear identity; you might say with personality. They make you feel there are real people in there somewhere.

Engage the user

What also tends to distinguish the sites you like is the feeling that they are meant for you or someone like you. Remember that the Web is interactive. As a writer, you need to engage the other person in the dialogue – the user. Your home page should sound as if it is starting a conversation. As in a conversation, you will want to introduce yourself and make the user feel welcome. 'Welcome' can be one of the most important words on a home page. You will almost certainly write in the first person as 'we' or even 'I' and the user will be 'you'. Even when you write in the third person, describing yourself or your organisation as 'they' or 'it', you should try to work in a 'you' every now and then to address the user directly.

The more clearly you can visualise your typical user, the better the conversation you will be able to construct. You will choose the right words to communicate with that person. Apart from using the appropriate language, one of the ways in which websites engage the user is by offering them the chance to adapt the site to their own requirements. This is one way in which sites belonging to big corporations or government departments can make their sites more friendly (Figure 12.1). Users don't necessarily take up the offer. Many people either can't be bothered or don't want to miss the possibility of chancing upon interesting information, but by making the offer you show you are trying.

Successful websites are often those that offer users the chance to receive email. This may be a regular newsletter or information tailored to individual users' interests, such as stories about particular topics or notice of certain events.

Figure 12.1 Offering the user the chance to personalise the site and receive emails.

Either way, the communication creates a relationship between the user and the site and makes the user feel it is worth the trouble to visit that site (Figure 12.2).

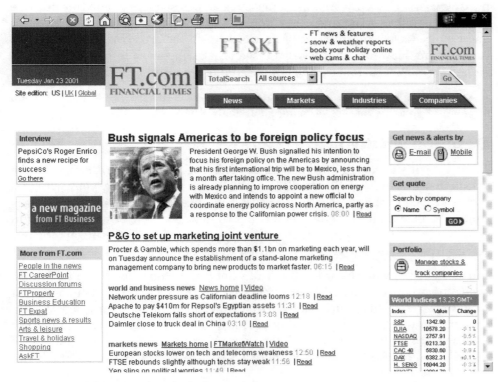

Figure 12.2 Offering emails and telephone messages.

Another way of engaging users is to invite them to contribute to the site, but you need to be careful. A home page that asks users for anything before it has given them something substantial in the way of information or enjoyment risks putting users off. Many organisations, such as newspapers, made this mistake when they first went on line. They were afraid of losing their existing business and required users to subscribe or at least register before giving them access to information. However, they soon realised that giving away information on line gained them new customers and enhanced their reputation with existing ones.

Asking people to register on the home page at all is likely to put some of them off, even if you say you are offering good deals (Figure 12.3).

Describe what you are offering

The next consideration is what you are offering. As I said in Chapter 3, the user's first question is 'What will this site do for me?' The way you write this part is crucial to the success of your site. You have a few lines in which to persuade the user that you have something they want. Your best chance lies in vivid but factual description, rather than hyperbole, and in writing about your service from the user's perspective rather than your own.

You also need to make clear the limits of what you are offering. If you tell people about the products you make, users may assume they can order them online. If they can't, you need to put in an address or telephone number high up the page, or mention writing or telephoning pretty quickly. You don't need to list the things you can't do, just think and choose your words carefully. For example, the Lawrights site (Figure 12.4) does not say 'We are sorry that we are unable to

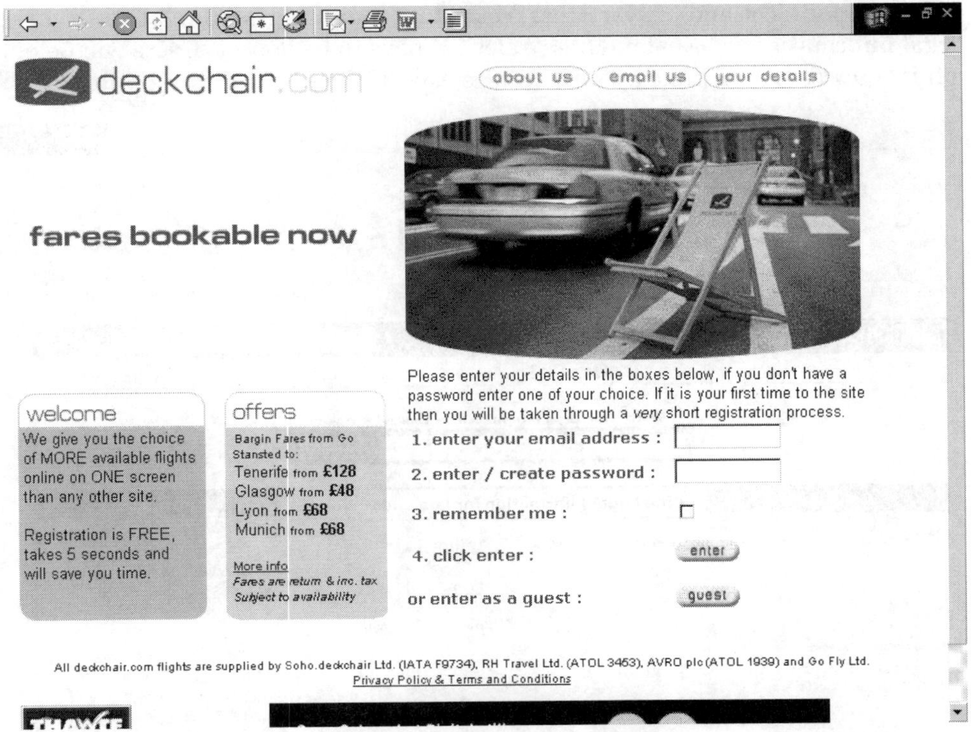

Figure 12.3 Asking people to register on the home page is likely to put some of them off.

help users in Scotland or Northern Ireland'. It simply says straight away 'Free legal information for England and Wales'. It pays to be honest. Users will be put off if you waste their time by raising false expectations.

Figure 12.4 Making clear the limits of what you are offering.

Describe how to get it

Having told users what they can expect from your site, you need to tell them how to get it. It helps to have a familiar navigation system used by other sites similar to your own. Research suggests that the value of familiarity outweighs the weakness of any particular system of navigation. You still need to explain the navigation, as briefly as you can. It is probably enough to say something like 'Choose one of the categories on the left to see ...' or 'Try our list of products from x to y'. You can't explain it in detail, but it is important that the home page should be an introduction to both the content and the workings of your site. The text should support the links by using the same words in the same order and reinforce the ideas represented by the links (Figure 12.5). The fewer the words you use, the more important it is to choose them well and use them consistently (Figure 12.6).

Place your links

Having links in the text as well as in a list helps to reinforce your links. It is a good idea to give the user more than one way of reaching other pages and you can explain a link in the text, but if you put links in the text you need to place them carefully and avoid cluttering the text with too many. That said, the home pages of some very successful sites, such as news sites, consist almost entirely of links in fairly dense text. I think they get away with it because they tend to come from known organisations and use familiar categories of information, and so have less need to explain themselves.

As a general rule, if you put links in sentences or paragraphs, make them unobtrusive. Underline one word or two, not whole phrases. Some Web writers refuse to put links in the text in case the user goes straight to another page and

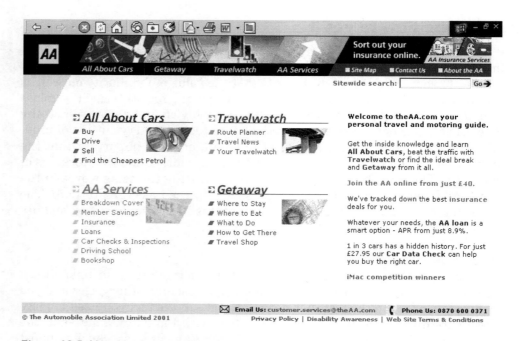

Figure 12.5 Using the same words in the text and the links.

Figure 12.6 If you use very few words, use them consistently, and in the same order.

misses the rest of the information in that sentence, paragraph or page. This is less likely if you place your links carefully, at the end of sentences and paragraphs, but you have to accept that you cannot dictate to the user. You cannot even guide. You can only offer. It is up to you to balance the value to users of having more than one way of getting to other pages against the value to you of being able to persuade them to read as much of what you have written as possible. Probably the sooner you abandon the idea that you are in charge, the better (Figure 12.7).

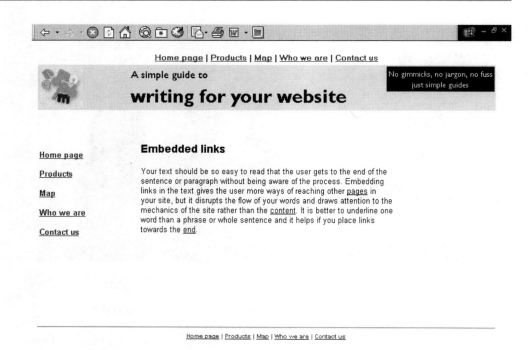

Figure 12.7 The pros and cons of embedding links in your text.

Write your links

Writing 'Click here to ...' is frowned on by many Web experts. You want to be helpful to inexperienced users, but you have to consider several objections to this device. One is that some users don't use a mouse and therefore don't click at all. Another is that it wastes words: not everyone will want to follow the link and you could use those words to give information and a link at the same time. A third objection is on visual grounds. 'Click here' links draw attention to the wrong words. If you have several of them on a home page, the user scanning for information sees a series of '<u>here</u>'s or '<u>click</u>'s instead of the categories of information you are offering (Figure 12.8).

The better you have planned your site and what you want to say, the more easily the links will integrate with the text and the less conscious the user will be of the mechanics of the site. Anticipating who will want to use your site and organising it accordingly makes for a home page that needs very little narrative (Figure 12.9).

When you are writing words that either lead to a link or support a link elsewhere on the page, put the offer first and the action required second. Otherwise the user may be presented with a rather mystifying instruction such as 'Press Ctrl+P to print map'. It is more helpful to the user the other way round, as 'To print map press Ctrl + P', or if you have space 'For your copy of the map, press Ctrl+P on your computer'. Besides, it is good psychology. If the user sees 'Scroll down to see examples of my work', there's always a danger that the response will be 'Why should I?'

Whenever you suggest that the user do something, give them a reason first. This is especially important when you ask them for information. If you tell the user why you need a postcode, for example, and what you will do with it, you are much more likely to get it. Most of us are not keen to give away personal

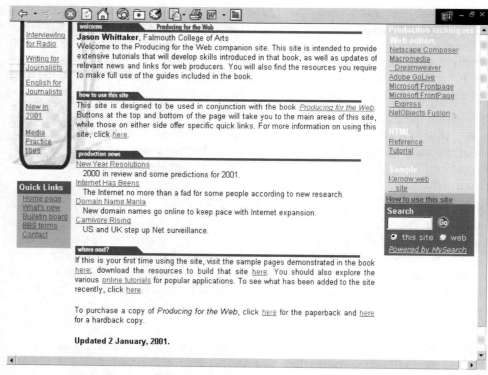

Figure 12.8 A profusion of 'here's' draws attention to the wrong words.

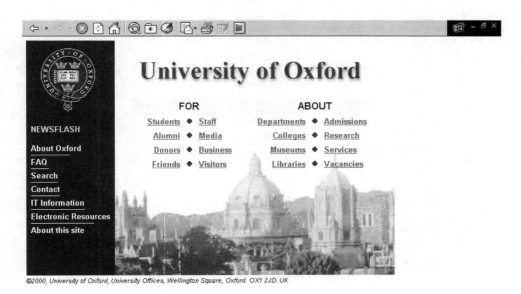

@2000, University of Oxford, University Offices, Wellington Square, Oxford. OX1 2JD. UK

Figure 12.9 Thinking who will want to use your site and for what produces a clean home page.

details on a website, still less to enable someone to use our credit card. If you are to persuade someone else to do so, you need to win the user's confidence, ask nicely and make it easy (Figure 12.10).

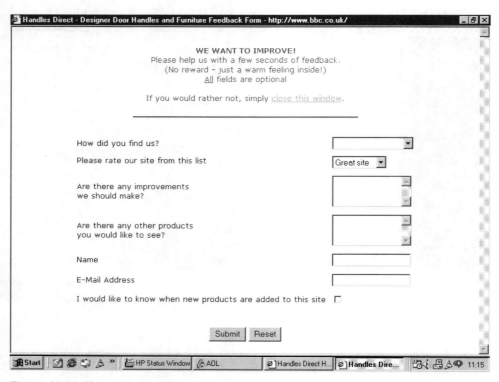

Figure 12.10 If you ask a user for information, tell them why and make it easy.

Invite contributions

Asking users for comments and contributions is a sign of confidence, but before you do you need to think about how you are going to handle them. You won't establish much of a relationship with users if you ask for suggestions and then ignore, misquote or ridicule them. For a start, be sure that you want contributions; otherwise it's better not to invite them. Then you need to tell people what you will do with them and stick to it or explain why, for example, you are not quoting contributions in full. You may make it easier for people by giving them a form to fill in. That would be on another page. On the home page, you will have room for only the briefest of invitations.

Put your best bits first

You have so much to put into so few words. You may find that the space you are working with is even smaller than you first thought. The top of the screen will be filled by the browser's menu bar, and some more of the top, and one side or some other part, will be taken up with navigation. It's worth remembering that some users will not have the screen maximised and many will not bother to scroll. So all your important words – who you are, what you are offering, how to use the site – must appear near the top of the screen. The prime space on a newspaper page is 'above the fold'. On a Web page, it is vital that your key messages are 'above the line.'

You have to put your best bits first. You are not writing a novel. Unlike Jane Austen, you cannot afford to write an intriguing introduction, keep your readers waiting a couple of chapters before introducing the hero and expect them to read to the end of the book to find out what happens to him. Writing a Web page is more like writing news stories. Give the most important point immediately and leave it to the users to find out more if they are interested. This is most true of your home page: if it doesn't grab the user straight away, your website is a waste of time.

Summary

Your home page must identify you and what you are offering in no more than 30 words.

You need to visualise your user and engage them as if in conversation.

It is a mistake to ask for information or commitment from a user straight away.

Your home page must persuade the user that you have something they want.

You should make clear what you are not offering, as well as what you are.

Introduce the navigation: make the text support the links.

Having links in the text helps to reinforce your links, but too many may confuse the user.

'Click here' should be used with care, if at all.

Give users a reason for doing something before asking them or telling them how to do it.

Invite contributions, but make sure you know, and say, what you are going to do with them.

All your important words should be visible to the user without scrolling.

Put your best bits first.

Writing summaries, headlines and lists

Summaries

Headlines

Lists

Bullet points

This chapter deals with three of the vital elements of Web writing: summaries, headlines and lists. It builds on the work you have done so far on writing concisely, understanding the structure of language and thinking about the visual impact of your words. It suggests ways of practising the skills dealt with here.

Summaries

To sum up a story in a few words is quite a daunting task, especially when you know it may be your only chance to get the information across. Your job may require you to write an executive summary of a long report or to write down on one sheet of paper everything a colleague needs to know for a meeting. Almost any writing involves summarising in some way. On a Web page, where you have so little space, it is a vital skill.

Gather your source material. This may be all in one form, such as a written report or article. It may be your memory of a conversation with one or more people, or notes from such a conversation or meeting. It may be a recording of an interview or something you are going to review. It may be a mixture of any of these. If you are going to tell someone else about it, you need to understand it yourself.

Ideally when you summarise, you should use the raw material rather than a version that has already been digested by someone else – a PR person, for example, or a news agency journalist – who may have reasons for interpreting it in a certain way. Such versions are intended to sell the material to a customer and often include persuasive introductions that are not borne out by the body of the report. In real life, it is often impossible to go back to original sources. We simply don't have time, but it is worth bearing in mind that summaries are just that – someone else's version.

When you have gathered your material, go through it for a general idea of what it is about. It is probably better not to take notes at this stage as you want to get a sense of the whole story. When you have got the gist of it, make a few notes from memory. Then go through it again carefully, making notes, under-lining or using a highlighter pen. Think what points you want to include and in what order. Plan what you are going to say.

When I was learning to write news, I was encouraged to put the source mater-ial away and write from memory. I still find it the best method. Writing from memory makes you assess and digest the information before you write. You then write confidently and produce a more natural, flowing summary because you are using your own words and keeping the shape of the whole piece in your head. Writing with your source material strewn around you can produce a cut-and-paste job that is stilted and unsatisfactory, because you tend to use other people's words and your attention is on details, so you can easily lose the thread of the piece. If you need to consult the source material to quote some-thing accurately, you can always mark your draft and carry on writing. When you have finished, you can go back to check that quotation or fact, and you should in any case go back to check that your summary is accurate.

Mixing the general and specific

There's a danger that in summarising you lose the elegance of the original, the detail and the colour. A summary that consists of generalisations is boring and uninformative. Lists of specifics can also be boring. Try to use an element of both – a general point with something specific that illustrates it. The general point tells readers what you are talking about and the specific gives them something they can visualise or identify with.

Practise summing up information in two sentences, say 30 words. That makes a nice short paragraph on a Web page.

Writing summaries is something journalists do all the time. The advantage journalists have is not so much talent or training – important though these are – as daily practice and criticism from editors and colleagues. The more you write and the more feedback you get on what you write, the better your writing is likely to be. Writing headlines is another journalistic skill that is essential for good Web writing. It, too, needs practice.

Headlines

Whereas a summary tells you what the story is, a headline tells you what is interesting about it. Headlines are sometimes described as enticing a reader into a story. There is a difference between enticing and teasing. A teaser does not tell you much and often does not deliver what it promises. This is annoying in any circumstances. On a website it can be disastrous. Users lose patience very quickly. Put yourself in their position. If you buy a newspaper or magazine, you are prepared to make some effort to read it. After all, you chose it and paid for it. Users have made no such decision about your site. They are investing their time, and it takes far more time and effort to look around a site than it does to find what you want in a magazine.

Observe your own behaviour in a website. Which links do you tend to follow? Do you tend to go for the informative headlines or the intriguing ones? It may depend on the type of site. If it is a site geared to hard information, clearly the informative ones are the more likely to work. But even in sites that are entertaining, you don't want to be disappointed or misled and you do not want to waste too much time as things on the Web take so much longer than they do on paper.

What about jokes and puns? Puns are a favourite device of headline-writers. At the risk of sounding stuffy, my advice is: avoid jokes and puns. That doesn't mean never use them, just don't try too hard. Jokes and puns make a lot of assumptions about the people you are writing for – that they have similar experiences, knowledge and sense of humour, in other words a similar culture. Such headlines are often appreciated by people who don't get the allusion, but that's because they sound good anyway. Your effort should go into writing something that sounds interesting. If you manage a joke or pun, it's a bonus.

To write an interesting headline, first think of a person you want to interest. It's easy enough to write something that amuses you; it's more important to interest the people you are writing for and it helps if you visualise them. Imagine yourself ringing someone up to tell them the story or going home to someone quite unconnected with your work and being asked about it, or talking to a stranger. Imagine yourself in a group where you have to take your turn in the conversation and you have a very short time to capture the interest of the most important person there. Whichever device is most appropriate, it helps to think of an individual and how you can make the story interesting to that person.

Do you write the story or the headline first? We often think of a clever headline before we have written the story and then find that the story we have written doesn't match the headline. You should write the story first and then think how you can attract someone to it with an appropriate headline. In practice, however, it doesn't much matter provided you always check the headline afterwards and rewrite it if it doesn't match. Starting with a headline, at least in mind, is often a way of launching ourselves into a story because it provides an angle. It gets us going.

Is the headline the same as the first sentence of the story? No. The first sentence is part of the story and will be written accordingly. It is rather boring to read a headline and then find that the first sentence of the story is exactly the same. The headline, ideally written afterwards, stands alone and should give the flavour of the story, the reason for reading it. The headline does not itself have to be a sentence, but it will be more informative if it is. It does have to be short as it has more impact if it is all on one line.

Headlines on websites have to work harder than they do in print. In newspapers and magazines, headlines often appear above the stories they refer to. On a website they are usually on one page and the stories they refer to are on separate pages. Your headlines have to make the user think it is worth the effort to follow a link to another page and risk losing himself in your site.

Headlines on one page also have to make sense as a group. In that, they are rather like the table of contents in this book. Having written the chapters, I went back to the Contents to see if the chapter headings made sense as a list. They had to be roughly the same length, and short but informative. They had to convey a sense of progress from the introduction to the conclusion. They had to form a balanced whole, being neither repetitive nor mismatched, not sounding as though they were put together in bits at different stages but written as a set.

On a website, your set of headlines will tend to be much shorter than the table of contents of a book, but they must make sense as a set as well as represent the stories they refer to. This applies also to side-headings. If you break up text into paragraphs, each with a side-heading, the side-headings should not only give the flavour of the paragraph they refer to but also make a coherent list. You will often highlight them in some way so that the user can scan the side-headings to find what interests him. In the next chapter, for example, the side-headings are Editing, Proofreading, Testing, Maintaining and Using old material. The last side-heading was originally Archive, making a list of five single words, which looked neat. On re-reading it, however, I thought it was more important to have a list of the same kinds of words and changed it to Using …

Lists

In our search for ways of writing pages that the user can scan easily for information, we have discussed breaking up text into paragraphs; writing summaries, headlines and side-headings; and making lists of headlines and side-headings. Now we'll look at two of the most useful devices on a website – lists of links and bullet points.

It's worth spending a little time thinking about how lists work. Putting information in a list is a way of making a lot of information accessible in a short time. A list can consist of almost anything – departments of an organisation, people in those departments, hobbies, actions required, qualities in a person, types of products and so on. The important characteristic of a list is that the items in it should be of the same type.

A shopping list consists of objects that you need to buy. If you put down apples, oranges, potatoes and cabbage, you have a coherent list of things you will probably buy in one place. If you add a couple of newspapers, anti-freeze and light bulbs, you will probably have to think of several different places to go, but you are still dealing with things you are going to buy. If you add 'wallpaper for kitchen', you are still dealing with something you want to buy, but it will presumably need more time and thought than buying potatoes. If you then add 'Book dentist appointment' and 'Must remember to ask Jo about the sunflowers', you are liable to get confused. Putting all these things in the same list makes it hard to use. You may well sort the items into separate lists. Alternatively, you may say 'It's my list, I know what it means'.

If you were to ask someone else to do your shopping, however, you would think far more carefully about what to put on the list and how you described those things. You might want to specify what kind of cabbage you needed and where the cheapest anti-freeze could be bought. On your website, your lists are all drawn up for someone else – the user. What is more, the user does not necessarily understand at first glance what a list consists of, unless you make it clear. This is hard when your lists are made up of single words, as are many lists of links.

I mentioned lists in Chapter 4 when we were talking about organising your site. I said three items were the minimum needed to make a list. If you write down two things, another person may see a connection between them, but it takes a third item to confirm that they have made the right connection. Most people can keep about seven items in their head at once. If your list goes up to nine or ten, you are making it hard for the user to understand what you are offering. Once you have more than seven items, you should think about putting them into separate categories (Figure 13.1).

The order you put the items in should be decided with the user in mind. Many lists you see on websites make no sense to the user. The items are in the order of their importance to the owner of the site rather than the user. Even when sites put items in the order they think they are most likely to be used, the logic is not necessarily obvious, certainly not to the first-time user. Once a list is longer than, say, five items, there is a lot to be said for making it alphabetical. At least the user can understand at a glance how the list works and may then feel more comfortable looking to see what it contains.

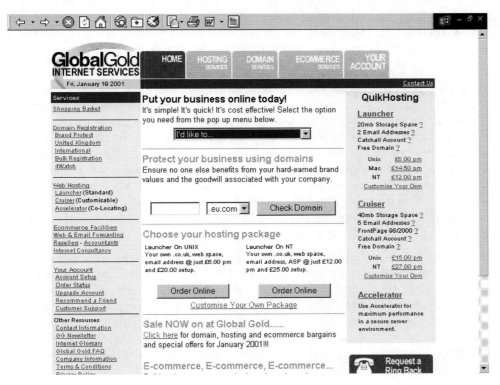

Figure 13.1 Dividing lists into categories.

Bullet points

Breaking up text into bulleted lists is only a little easier than writing lists of links. Putting a mark in front of short bits of text and putting the bits on separate lines may make the page look orderly, but the bullet points won't work unless the contents have been carefully thought out. Keep in mind the idea of a shopping list. That will focus your attention on the things to be listed rather than the appearance of a list (Figure 13.2).

Badly written bullet points are those that are not real lists, because they consist of things that are not the same and so cannot be understood at a glance. They will be more difficult to read than a well written paragraph. Real lists consist of ideas expressed in the same way. That means using the same part of speech – five nouns or noun phrases, for example, or five adjectives. A list of things to do would consist of verbs 'fetch dry cleaning, book appointment with dentist, check diaries with Sarah, order paper for printer', expressed in the same way, in this case in the imperative. If you were to add a fifth item, 'I must remember to ring Mum', it would no longer be a real list, but if you changed that item to 'ring Mum', it would.

As the purpose of a bulleted list is to enable the user to scan a lot of information in a small space, your items should not go over one line. They may be short sentences, but they usually work best if they are single words or phrases, with an introduction (Figure 13.3). They should be of similar length to look tidy and be easy to scan (Figure 13.4). I suggest that bullet points should start in lower case, unless of course they are proper names, because the bullet, like the capital letter, is a device for drawing attention. If you use two such devices at once, you tend to confuse the reader.

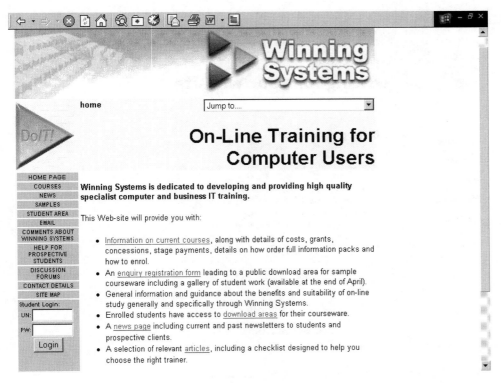

Figure 13.2 Bullet points that are not real lists are hard to follow.

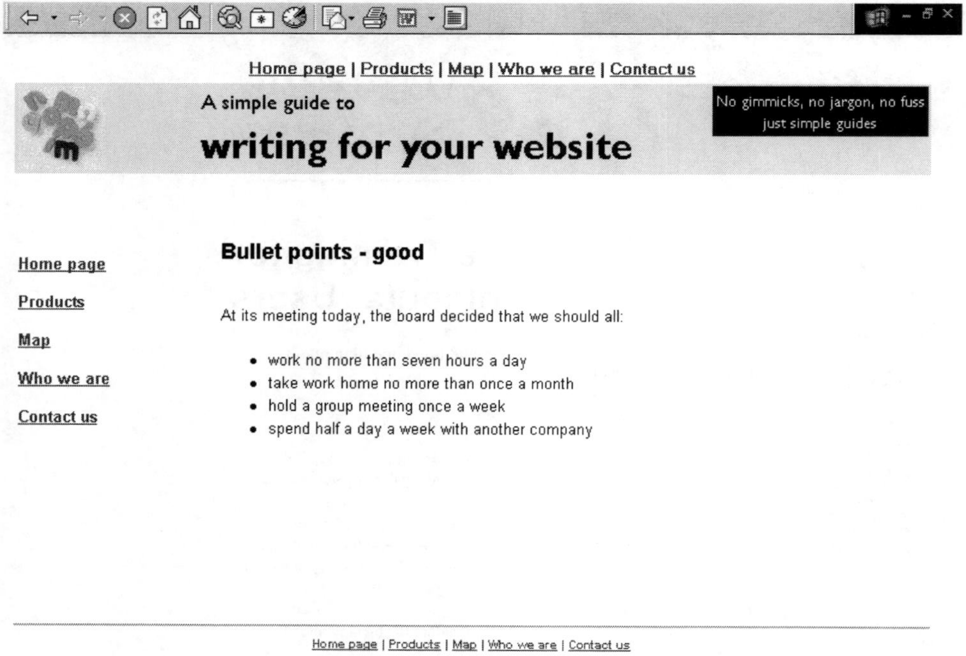
Home page | Products | Map | Who we are | Contact us
A simple guide to
writing for your website
No gimmicks, no jargon, no fuss
just simple guides
Home page
Products
Map
Who we are
Contact us
Bullet points - good
At its meeting today, the board decided that we should all:
• work no more than seven hours a day
• take work home no more than once a month
• hold a group meeting once a week
• spend half a day a week with another company
Home page | Products | Map | Who we are | Contact us

Figure 13.3 Real lists consist of ideas expressed in the same way.

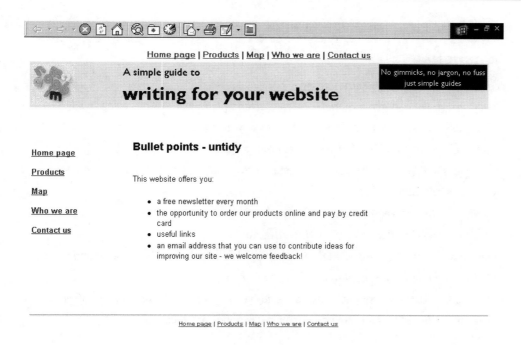

Figure 13.4 Bullet points of varying lengths are hard to scan.

The bullet is a powerful visual device. Make sure that the information you put in a bulleted list is really important and not just the bits that are easy to put into a list. Otherwise you will distort your message.

It's worth taking some time to practise converting text into bullet points.

Summary

Almost all writing involves summarising.

Read through your source material, make notes and plan what you are going to say.

Write from memory, then go back and look at anything you need to check.

A mixture of general points and specific examples makes a good summary.

Headlines should arouse the user's interest in a story, without exaggerating or misleading.

Avoid jokes and puns.

Visualise the person you are trying to interest.

Write the headline after you have written the story.

Headlines on websites have to work harder than they do in print: they often stand alone.

Headlines on one page should make sense as a set.

Lists of links must make sense to the user and be written from the user's point of view.

Bullet points should be real lists and lists of really important things.

Editing and maintaining

Editing

Proofreading

Testing

Maintaining

Using old material

This chapter deals with the last stages of writing and gives you some advice about maintaining your site.

Editing

All good writers read and re-read and edit their work. No one expects to get everything right first time. Editing is a sign of strength, not weakness.

Do it on paper. You shouldn't be surprised by that advice. We've said all along that reading on a screen is difficult. You have geared your writing to a user who will scan your text on screen and very likely print anything they need to read in detail. By the same token, you will edit and proofread better if you print your text and scrutinise it with pen or pencil in hand. You will also find it easier to move the pages about and compare them when you can see them all in one go.

Better still, get a second person to read your text as well. You are familiar with the material by now. Words that seem clear to you may not be clear to someone reading them for the first time. You may have explained something that another person finds obvious or left out something they think needs explaining. A second pair of eyes brings a fresh view. Asking for a second opinion reminds you that people understand things differently and that your writing can always be improved.

Read it through for sense. You may decide you've left out an important piece of information. You may think some ideas make better sense in a different order. You may rewrite whole chunks. If you make changes, big or small, be sure to check the text that comes before and after. Make sure that the writing flows smoothly from the old to the new and into the old again.

Proofreading

When you're happy with the shape of it, test every word to make sure it is needed. If you can say the same thing more briefly, do. Check for correct use of words, grammar and punctuation. Make sure you use the same words, spellings and punctuation to say the same things on different pages. Check that the wording of the links matches the headings of the pages they lead to: don't have a link saying 'About us' leading to a page headed 'Who we are'. Even more than on a printed page or between pages of a book, the effect of inconsistency is jarring when you can click from one page to another so quickly.

Make a note of key words and phrases that you use on your site so that you can make sure they appear the same way everywhere. These notes can be the basis of a style guide for your site. You may find this helpful to refer to when you are adding to or rewriting pages. If more than one person is writing in the site, it is essential.

Testing

As well as editing and proofreading your pages on paper, you need to test the pages on screen. As there is no fixed order to the pages, it is important to check them from every possible direction to see that they make sense in every case. Get someone else to test them as well. You can also check that the words that come up in alt tags and rollovers, if you use them, match those on the page. If you make changes at this stage, you should proofread the pages again.

Maintaining

You launch your site. It works. Everything is fine, but you cannot relax. A website is not a printed publication that, once out, you cannot change. Users know you have the means to change it at any time and they expect it to be fresh and up-to-date. How up-to-date will depend on the kind of site it is but your business, your organisation or your life is bound to change and your website will need to reflect that change. Whatever you are offering, you have started a dialogue with users and your site cannot be static. One way of developing it is to use any comments or contributions you have invited: after all, you are getting material for nothing. Maintaining a website is rather like gardening. Sooner or later, you will need to do some weeding or pruning or planting; dig up some areas and replace them; or perhaps re-design the whole thing. Your website doesn't grow on its own, but if left alone for too long it may appear to wilt or even die.

Using old material

One last word – recycling. The compost that enriches the Web is old material. One of the greatest advantages of the Web over other media is that yesterday's words are just as accessible as today's. This won't be relevant for all sites, but for many it is worth rewriting old material and re-presenting it as Archive, or whatever you choose to call it, and making it available indefinitely. After all, there is no shortage of space.

Summary

Read your text through on paper and edit it.

Get a second person to read it too.

Check for omissions, repetition, redundant words and mistakes in grammar or spelling.

Check for consistency of style throughout your site.

Test your pages on screen from every direction.

Maintain your site as if it were a garden.

Sources

Books

A Plain English Handbook, Office of Investor Education and Assistance, Securities and Exchange Commission, 1998.

Politics and the English Language in *A Collection of Essays*, George Orwell, Harcourt Brace, 1981.

Broadcast News Writing, Reporting and Producing, Ted White, Focal Press, 1996.

Designing Web Usability, Jakob Nielsen, New Riders, 1999.

Information Architecture for the World Wide Web, Louis Rosenfeld & Peter Morville, O'Reilly, 1998.

Our Masters' Voices, Max Atkinson, Routledge, 1984.

Producing for the Web, Jason Whittaker, Routledge, 2000.

Teach Yourself Correct English, B.A. Phythian, Hodder & Stoughton, 1985.

The Complete Plain Words, Sir Ernest Gowers, HMSO/Penguin, 1973.

The Elements of Style, William Strunk Jr & E.B. White, Allyn and Bacon, 2000.

The Real Thing, Tom Stoppard, Faber and Faber, 1982.

The Right Way to Write, Rupert Morris, Piatkus, 1998.

The Right Word at the Right Time, Reader's Digest, The Reader's Digest Association, 1985.

The Story of English, Robert McCrum, Robert MacNeil, William Cran, Faber and Faber/BBC Books, 1986.

Use Your Head, Tony Buzan, BBC Books, 1974.

Web Style Guide, Patrick J.Lynch & Sarah Horton, Yale University Press, 1999.

Wired Words, Steve Morris, ft.com, 2000.

Words and Rules, Steven Pinker, Phoenix, 1999.

Writing for the Web, Crawford Kilian, Self-Counsel, 1999.

Writing for Journalists, Wynford Hicks, Routledge, 1999.

Articles

'Sense and nonsense', Bryan Magee, *Prospect* magazine, February 2000.

'Sex on the Net', Nicholas Thompson, *Prospect* magazine, January 2001, originally published in *The Washington Monthly*.

Websites

alertbox	Jakob Nielsen	useit.com
Poynter Institute	Poynter Institute	poynter.org
The Web Writer	Jennifer Kyrnin	http://html.about.com
WebPagesThatSuck	Vincent Flanders	WebPagesThatSuck.com

Broadcasts

The Routes of English	Melvyn Bragg	BBC Radio 4
The Long View: Trial by Jury	Jonathan Freedland	BBC Radio 4

Acknowledgements

Thanks to Clare Brigstocke at the BBC who started me training people to write for websites; to Rupert Morris of Clarity who persuaded me to write this book and provided helpful criticism of more than one draft; to Christopher Clarke for his comments on the text and to Julia Swann, Mel Leggett and Rob Young for their help with the illustrations.

I am grateful to the following for allowing me to use their Web pages, many of which have changed since the time of writing, as illustrations:

AA	theaa.com
Amazon	amazon.com and amazon.co.uk
Tonia Billiot	geocities.com/tonia_billiot/CHEETAHS.html
Cabinet Office	servicefirst.gov.uk
deckchair.com	deckchair.com
Mike Donovan, editor of Practical Farm Ideas	farmideas.co.uk
Ford Motor Company	ford.co.uk
Foreign and Commonwealth Office	fco.gov.uk
FT	ft.com

Global Gold	globalgold.co.uk
Handles Direct	handlesdirect.co.uk
Lawrights	lawrights.co.uk
London Clinic	lonclin.co.uk
Morgan Stanley Dean Witter	msdw.com
Oxford University	ox.ac.uk
Jason Whittaker, author of Producing for the Web	producing.routledge.com
Winning Systems	winsys.co.uk

and to Faber & Faber for permission to quote from The Real Thing by Tom Stoppard, The Buzan Centres for permission to use a Mind Map® and Mr D.C. Raitby of The Hardware Shop in Woodstock for letting me use his shop as an example.

Index